THE HOW AND WHY WONDER BOOK OF
The MICROSCOPE
AND WHAT YOU SEE

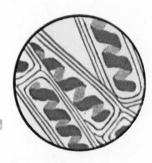

Written by MARTIN KEEN

Illustrated by WALTER FERGUSON

Editorial Production: DONALD D. WOLF

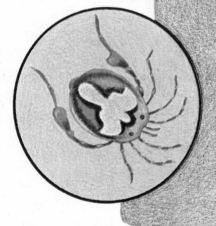

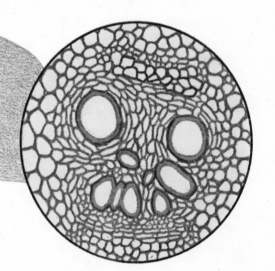

Edited under the supervision of
Dr. Paul E. Blackwood
Washington, D. C.

Text and illustrations approved by
Oakes A. White
Brooklyn Children's Museum
Brooklyn, New York

GROSSET & DUNLAP • **Publishers** • **NEW YORK**

Introduction

The How and Why Wonder Book of the Microscope introduces one of the instruments that has been most important to scientists in their never-ending search for accurate knowledge about our world. The instrument helps our eyes, wonderful as they are, to be even more wonderful, by extending the sense of sight. It brings before our eyes the world of invisible life, the world of tiniest plants and animals, the *bacteria* and *protozoa*. Indeed, the microscope makes the "unseen world" visible.

But to get full pleasure and benefit from this remarkable instrument requires knowledge of how to operate it carefully. It requires practice in focusing light and in preparing specimens for examination. This book will help the beginning *microscopist* learn these things. And it gives directions for using the microscope to observe the details of many common things all around us. A page of this book suddenly becomes a mass of stringy fibers, while the surface of a tree leaf becomes a miracle of designs when viewed through a microscope.

Every young scientist has ahead of him many exciting experiences exploring the unseen world. *The How and Why Wonder Book of the Microscope,* like the other publications in the series, is a useful teacher and guide in that exploration.

Paul E. Blackwood

Dr. Blackwood is a professional employee in the U. S. Office of Education. This book was edited by him in his private capacity and no official support or endorsement by the Office of Education is intended or should be inferred.

Library of Congress Catalog Card Number: 61-1804

Contents

An Unseen World

The human eye is a wonderful organ. Our eyes tell us more about the world around us than any of our other sense organs do. The size and shape of things, their color, their distance from us, and whether one object is in front or in back, above or below, are all things we learn by using our eyes. We can see things that are only a few inches in front of our eyes, and then we can look out the window and instantly see things more than a mile away.

Yet, remarkable as our eyes may be, there are many things they cannot enable us to see. Among these are very small things. Usually, when we talk about small things, we mean things about the size of the period at the end of this sentence. Now, you can see the period quite easily, and if it were only one-tenth its size, you could still see it. But if the period shrank to one-hundredth of its present size, you would probably lose sight of it. Yet, small as the shrunken period might be, it would still be much larger than millions of

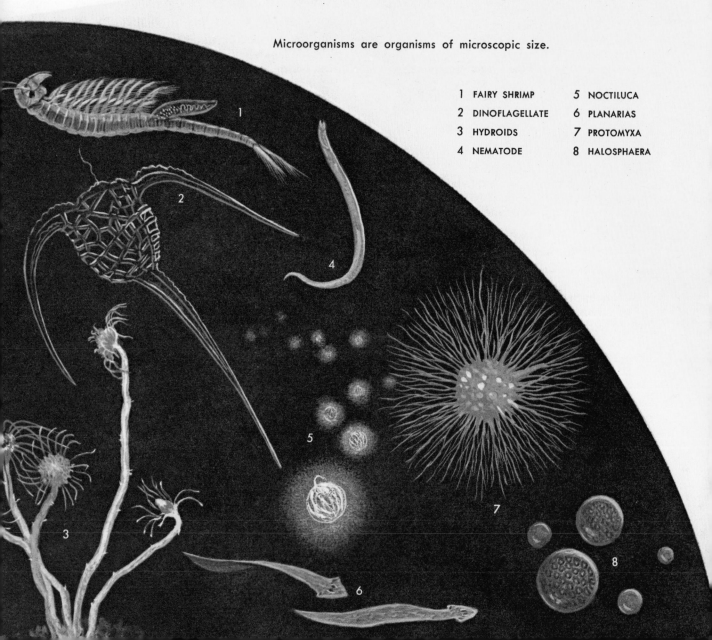

Microorganisms are organisms of microscopic size.

1 FAIRY SHRIMP	5 NOCTILUCA
2 DINOFLAGELLATE	6 PLANARIAS
3 HYDROIDS	7 PROTOMYXA
4 NEMATODE	8 HALOSPHAERA

different kinds of things that exist in your everyday world.

There are certain plants — which we shall soon learn about — that are so small you could put 250,000 of them on the period at the end of this sentence. And there are animals that are not much bigger.

No matter how closely you look at the sheet of paper on which these words are printed, it will still look like a fairly smooth surface, but if your eyes could see much smaller things than they naturally can, you would see that the paper is really a twisted mass of fibers.

There are hundreds of details about the world that are too small for your unaided eyes to see. How, then, do we

learn about these details? What can we use to aid our eyes in seeing the unseen world of very small things that are all around us? We can use an instrument called a *microscope*.

The Microscope

A microscope is an instrument for looking at small things.

What is a microscope?

The word *microscope* comes from two ancient Greek words, *mikros*, which means "small," and *skopein,* which means "to look at."

All microscopes have one thing in common: They contain one or more parts called *lenses.* A lens is any clear substance that has a definite shape and will bend light rays as they pass through it. Most lenses are made of glass, but a lens could be made of water, of oil, or of clear plastic.

When we see anything, we do so because light is reflected

How does it work?

from the object to our eyes. If the rays of light come straight from the object to our eyes, we see the object in its natural size. But if the rays of light coming to our eyes are bent in a certain way, then the object looks bigger. When this happens, we say the object is *magnified*. A lens of the proper shape can bend light, so that things we see through the lens are magnified. Any lens that does this is a microscope.

You may wonder if lenses can also

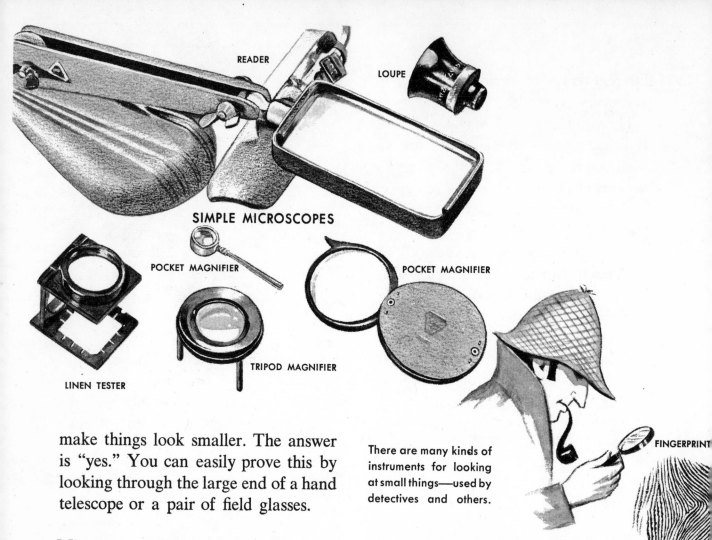

make things look smaller. The answer is "yes." You can easily prove this by looking through the large end of a hand telescope or a pair of field glasses.

There are many kinds of instruments for looking at small things—used by detectives and others.

What is a simple microscope? Microscopes that are made of one, or perhaps two, lenses are usually called *magnifying glasses,* or *hand lenses.* These are proper names for them, but they are also microscopes. Have you ever seen the magnifying glass used by stamp collectors? It is made up of just one or two small lenses fixed in a metal frame and held in the hand of the person using it. Have you ever seen a jeweler or a watchmaker looking at a gem or a watch through a black, snouty-looking object held at one eye? This is a microscope called a *loupe.* Did you ever see a picture of the detective Sherlock Holmes holding a round magnifying glass fixed in a circular band of metal and attached to a short handle? All

these are examples of *simple microscopes.* A simple microscope is one that is made up of one or more lenses that show you a magnified object right-side-up and in the same place where you would see it without the lens. You will understand this definition better when we learn about the other kind of microscope.

You can buy a single- or double-lens microscope in almost any toy store or five-and-ten-cent store. Such microscopes range in price from less than a dollar to three or four dollars. The very cheap ones may have poorly-made glass lenses or plastic lenses that scratch easily. A dollar and a half is probably the price for which you can buy a very useful hand lens, such as is used by stamp collectors.

When you have obtained your simple microscope, you can use it to learn things about your daily world that you never knew before. Obtain a magazine with a smooth, or slick, paper cover that bears the color photograph of a person. The majority of the slick paper magazines have covers like this. With your microscope, examine the face of the person in the picture. You will see that the color of the flesh of the face is made up of many tiny dots or specks of different colors. There are red, yellow, and green or blue dots, and the white color of the page shows through in spaces no bigger than the colored dots. Take the magnifying lens away and look at the page with your unaided eye. You will see how the combination of these dots, too small to be seen without the microscope, blends together to produce the color of flesh.

What can you see with a simple microscope?

With the microscope, look at the red area of the cheek or at the lips. You will see that there are more red dots crowded closer together in order to produce the redder color.

Open your handkerchief and look at it as you hold it up to the light. You can easily see that it is woven of thou-

A swatch of wool under a microscope shows its weave.

Cotton gabardine twill as viewed under a microscope.

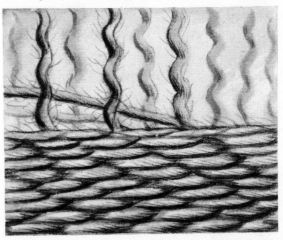

Newspaper print looks like this when it is magnified.

sands of threads. Now use your microscope to look at the handkerchief. You will see how each thread is woven, first under, then over, the threads near it. Note that all the threads are not equally thick. You will see that most of the threads look fuzzy because from their sides tiny, frayed filaments of fiber stick out.

Look at several different samples of

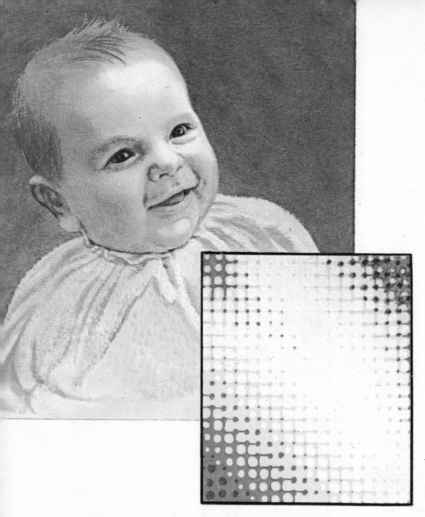

Amethyst crystal when magnified.

When you look at this print of a baby under a microscope, you can see that it is made up of many dots.

cloth that have colored patterns. How can you tell which samples have the color printed on them and which have the color woven into them? You can do this by tracing a single thread with your microscope. If, as far as you can follow the thread, it is one color, then the cloth has a woven pattern. On the other hand, if you trace a single thread and find that it is colored differently in different parts of the pattern, then the pattern was printed on the cloth.

Your microscope will reveal hundreds of new things, if you carefully examine the objects of your daily world. Examine a stone that has different colors in it. Look at the small hairs on the back of your hand. Examine a piece of wood along the surface where a carpenter has sawed it. Look at the leg of an insect.

You will add greatly to your interest and knowledge when working with a microscope, if you keep a record of what you see. You can keep such a record in a notebook or on file cards that are five inches long and three inches wide. Both the notebook and the cards can be bought in almost any stationery or five-and-ten-cent store.

How can you keep a record of what you see?

Here are the things to put in your record book or cards:

Examination number . . .
Date of examination . . .
Object examined . . .
Where I found it . . .
What I saw . . .
Remarks . . .

Under remarks, you might want to

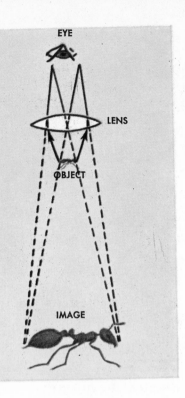

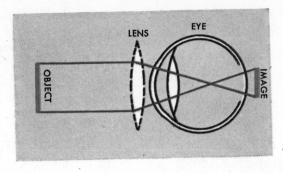

An image out of focus (left).

Image now in focus (right).

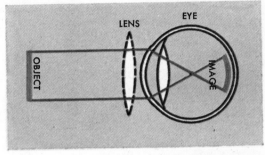

Diagram (left): light passing through simple microscope.

write something like: "Compare this with Examination number ____." For example, you may have just examined the antenna of a butterfly, and some time before, you had examined the antenna of a moth. You would probably want to make note of the fact that the antennas of these two kinds of insects are quite different. So, on the card bearing your record of the examination of the butterfly's antenna, you refer to the card bearing the record of the examination of the moth's antenna; and on the moth's card, you refer to the butterfly. Cross-references like this will greatly increase your knowledge of the things you examine.

When you were examining things with your simple microscope, you probably noticed that you could not see clearly when you held the lens just any old distance from the object. You had to move the lens back and forth until the object became clear. Why was this necessary?

What is a focus?

Your eye has a lens. This lens covers the part of your eye that is colored and also the dark spot, the pupil, at its center. Like all lenses, the one in your eye bends rays of light. The light is bent so that it falls on the back of your eye where light-sensitive materials are located. When the lens in your eye works just right, it bends light so that each light ray entering your eye from an object falls exactly in the proper place to give a sharp image of the object on the back of the eye. As long as the point where the light rays form a sharp image is exactly on the back of the eye, we see the object sharply and clearly. If this point is too far forward or too far back, objects we see are fuzzy and blurred. This is what happens to near- and far-sighted persons. The point at which a lens forms a sharp image is called the *focus* of the lens.

The lens of your microscope also has a focus. You had to move the microscope back and forth until the focus of its lens was exactly where it could work

9

with the lens in your eye, so as to form a sharp image on the back of your eye. We call the moving back and forth of a lens to form a sharp image *focusing* the lens.

With a pair of pliers, straighten out a

How can you make a water-lens microscope?

paper clip or a piece of wire of similar thickness. At one end of the wire, bend a complete loop about one-sixteenth of an inch across. Rub a little grease or cooking oil on the loop. Dip the loop in water and gently remove it. Within the loop will be a drop of water that forms a lens. Look at the print on a page through the water lens. The lens will probably magnify the print to twice its natural size. Eventually, the water will evaporate, but it is easy to make another water lens.

A different kind of microscope with

a water lens can also be made. With a heavy shears, cut a strip from a tin can. This tin strip should be about one inch wide and four inches long. Be careful not to cut yourself on the sharp edges of the tin. When the strip is cut, dull the edges with a file, or cover the edges with adhesive tape.

Mark the exact center of the tin strip. Place the strip on a piece of wood, and drive a medium-size nail through the center. Do not use a nail that will make a hole more than one-sixteenth inch in diameter. Remove the nail and the piece of wood.

Bend the ends of the strip downward, so that the strip will stand. As with the loop microscope, rub a little grease or oil around the hole in the strip. Stand the strip on its two ends. Dip a pencil in water and carefully remove it. Transfer a drop of water from the end of the pencil to the hole, so that a drop hangs in the hole, forming a lens.

Place a small pane of window glass on the tops of two tin cans of the same

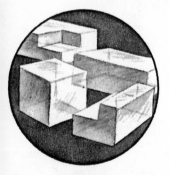

SALT CRYSTALS
MAGNIFIED

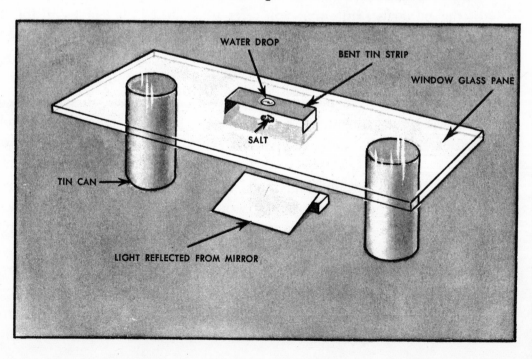

WATER DROP

BENT TIN STRIP

WINDOW GLASS PANE

SALT

TIN CAN

LIGHT REFLECTED FROM MIRROR

The first microscopist was Antony van Leeuwenhoek, a cloth merchant from Holland. He is pictured here with the microscope of his design. (b. 1632; d. 1723)

size. Place the tin strip carefully on the center of the glass. Beneath the glass, prop a flat mirror, such as is found in lady's handbags, so that light is reflected upward through the glass and the water lens.

Beneath the lens, place a few grains of pepper, salt, or sugar, and look down through the lens. Focus the lens by gently pressing on the strip. How many times do you think the water lens magnified the grains?

We don't know just who made the first
Who invented the microscope? microscope. In the thirteenth century, a monk named Roger Bacon learned how to grind glass to make spectacles. A little while afterward, gentlemen carried about with them a small microscope that consisted of a metal tube, about the size of your thumb, with a lens at one end. These were called flea glasses or fly glasses, and these names show pretty well what these microscopes were used for.

Although we do not know who invented
What is a microscopist? the microscope, we do know who was the first *microscopist*. A microscopist is a person who uses a microscope to study small things in a careful and systematic way. If you study things carefully with your simple microscope and keep a record of your findings, you are a microscopist. The first microscopist was Antony van Leeuwenhoek.

Van Leeuwenhoek was a cloth merchant who lived in Delft, Holland during most of the seventeenth century and part of the eighteenth. He lived a quiet life as a tradesman, but he was, in his spare time, one of the world's great scientific discoverers.

11

He obtained diamond dust from the diamond cutters of Delft with which he ground a nearly-spherical lens. He mounted the lens on a device that included a metal rod into which a screw-thread was cut. By turning the rod, he could make very fine focusing adjustments for his lens. The lens and the focusing device were both attached to a metal plate that had a hole in it, just below the lens. By placing objects beneath the hole, van Leeuwenhoek could magnify them as much as 300 times their natural size.

How was diamond dust used for a microscope?

GRASS SEEDLING

He was fascinated by the world of tiny things that his microscope opened up for him, and spent hours examining all sorts of things around him and writing careful reports on what he saw. He put many of his reports into letters that he sent to the Royal Society of London, an association made up of scientists. The scientists marveled at what van Leeuwenhoek wrote. They honored him by making their own microscopes and imitating his observations.

LOUSE

He hired an illustrator, called a limner, who joined him in his observations and then made drawings of what they both saw. One time van Leeuwenhoek put a louse under his microscope. This little animal was too active to observe well, so van Leeuwenhoek removed its head. However, the louse's legs kept kicking for more than an hour. Meanwhile, as van Leeuwenhoek wrote in his notes, "the Limner could not admire the sight enough, and it took him a long time to put his hand to paper."

GRASS SPIKELET

He studied the eyes of a shrimp, codfish, whale, rabbit, cow, and beetle. He studied the eggs of ants and lice. Seeds, blossoms, fruits, and other parts of the plant; the circulation of blood in the tail of a fish; the tartar on the teeth of an eight-year-old boy and two ladies; vinegar eels, crabs, and oyster eggs — all these were among the things van Leeuwenhoek placed beneath his microscope.

What objects did he study?

When he was eighty-five, he discovered that "some hundreds of nerves equal the size of a single hair of a man's beard!" And when he was past ninety, he was studying "the wonderful perfections and formations" in the eye of a fly.

With his simple microscope, his careful work, and his enthusiasm, Antony van Leeuwenhoek opened up a world that eventually led to the conquest of many diseases and an understanding of how the many things in the world are constructed.

The Compound Microscope

When most people hear the word "microscope," they usually think of the kind that is seen in laboratories. This microscope, as seen from the outside, has a heavy metal foot, a platform on which to place what is being examined, a nosepiece that points at the platform, and a long tube

What is a compound microscope?

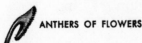

ANTHERS OF FLOWERS

Part of a feather magnified (below); how light rays pass through a compound microscope (right); a compound microscope (far right) with its parts indicated.

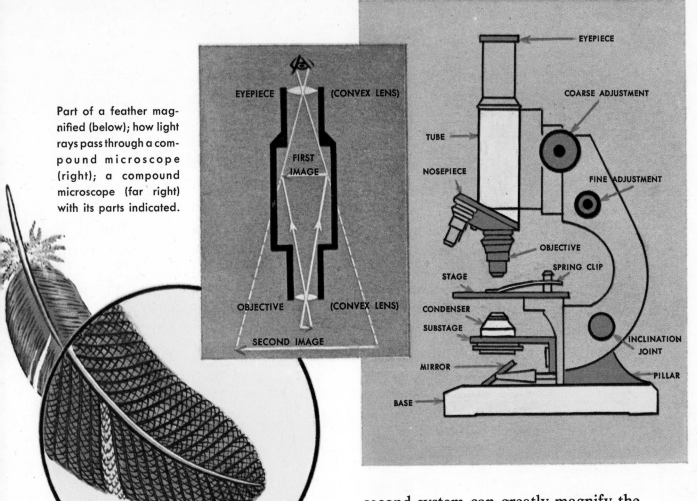

EYEPIECE (CONVEX LENS)

FIRST IMAGE

OBJECTIVE (CONVEX LENS)

SECOND IMAGE

EYEPIECE

COARSE ADJUSTMENT

TUBE

NOSEPIECE

FINE ADJUSTMENT

OBJECTIVE

STAGE

SPRING CLIP

CONDENSER

SUBSTAGE

INCLINATION JOINT

MIRROR

PILLAR

BASE

second system can greatly magnify the image and locate it just at the platform of the microscope.

Let us examine the compound laboratory microscope in order to learn its parts. First, let us examine the part through which light passes. Right above the platform, which is properly called the *stage*, is a narrow tube that contains lenses. This tube is called the *objective*. The microscope may have only one objective that fits into a wider tube, called the *nosepiece*. However, most laboratory microscopes have two or three objectives attached to a rotating nosepiece. With this arrangement, the microscopist need only turn

What are some parts of a compound microscope?

at the top of which the microscopist places his eye. This kind of microscope is called a *biological microscope,* or a *laboratory microscope*. It is also a *compound microscope*.

In a compound microscope, there are many lenses. These lenses are grouped into two systems. One system does exactly what a simple microscope does — it shows an upright image, just as the eye would see it, only larger. The focus of this set of lenses is at a point where the

What are the two systems of lenses?

the nosepiece to the right location in order to bring into use the objective he wants.

You may wonder why a microscope would have more than one objective. Each objective has a different magnifying power. The microscopist chooses the objective which magnifies that amount which best enables him to observe what he is looking at. If you look closely at the objectives of a laboratory microscope, you will see marked on one 10x, on the second 43x, and on the third 97x. The "x" means "times" and stands for just what it does in multiplication. An objective with 43x on it means that its lenses will magnify 43 times natural size.

Above the nosepiece, is a wide *tube*. It

How do you find out the magnifying power of a microscope?

is usually empty, but sometimes one or two special lenses are within the tube. Fitting into the upper part of it is a narrower tube called the *extension tube*. This one contains lenses. The lenses in the upper portion together make up the *eyepiece*, or *ocular*. On the ocular, you will see its magnifying power marked. Usually, this is 5x or 10x. If you use a 10x ocular with a 43x objective, the microscope has a total magnifying power of 10 x 43, or 430. In short, to know what the magnifying power of a microscope is, you multiply the power of the ocular by the power of the objective.

The parts of the microscope you have

What are the other parts of a compound microscope?

just learned are the most important, but it would be hard to use them without the other parts of a modern microscope. At the bottom of the microscope, is a broad, heavy metal *base*, sometimes called the *foot*. This base holds the working parts of the microscope steady. Rising from the back of the base is the *pillar*. This, too, holds the microscope steady, but at the top of the pillar is a joint, the *inclination joint*, that allows the upper part of the microscope to be tilted backward and forward. The large curved part that does the tilting is called the *arm*. The upper end of the arm holds the tube, while the lower end holds the *stage*. Affixed to the stage are two strips of springy steel. They are called *clips*, and their task is to hold specimens on the stage, especially when the stage is tilted. On more expensive microscopes, the stage is made in two layers. The upper layer can be moved forward or backward, or to the right or left, by turning pairs of knobs.

Where the tube meets the arm is a very important mechanism — the *adjustment*. There is a *coarse adjustment* and a *fine adjustment*. You remember the screw-threaded rod that van Leeuwenhoek fitted to his simple microscope. The coarse and the fine adjustments both consist of very accurately machined screw threads, by means of

GLOEOCAPSA

SCENADESMUS

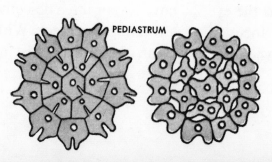

PEDIASTRUM

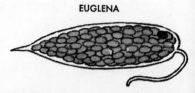

EUGLENA

which the tubes and objectives can be raised and lowered, in order to focus the microscope.

At the very bottom of the arm, a *mirror* is affixed, so that a beam of light can be shined up, through a hole in the stage, to the bottom of the objective, and from there, through the tubes to the eyepiece. Between the mirror and the stage, some microscopes have a third system of lenses to better concentrate the light from the mirror. This system is called a *substage condenser*.

Suppose you wish to examine a hair from your head. First, place on the stage a *glass slide,* which is a piece of clear glass one inch

How do you use a laboratory compound microscope?

wide and three inches long, and about half as thick as window glass. Push the slide under the clips, so that it is' held firmly. Then cut a one-inch length of hair and place it on the slide right above the hole in the stage. Your breath might easily blow the hair away, so fix it in place. This is best done with a material called *Canada balsam.* However, if you have no balsam, use clear household cement or clear fingernail polish.

Put a small drop of balsam on top of the hair. Wait a few moments in the hope that any tiny bubbles in the balsam will rise to the surface and burst. Don't wait too long, for Canada balsam (and household cement and fingernail polish) harden in air. So gently place on the balsam a very thin piece of glass, about one inch square, called a *cover glass* or *cover slip*. If you see bubbles beneath the cover glass, gently press down upon the cover glass with the tip of a pair of tweezers or a tooth pick. This should help to expel the bubbles. Now the hair is properly *mounted.*

Next, take care of the lighting. To do this, look at the stage from the side, and with the coarse adjustment, move the bottom of the objective to a point about one-sixteenth of an inch above the cover glass. If the microscope has more than one objective, use the one with the lowest magnifying power. When the objective is positioned close to the slide, look into the eyepiece. With one hand, move the mirror about until you see a bright, evenly-lit circle of light, not glaring, not dim. Now you are ready to focus.

Preparing a slide for the microscope properly will make viewing easier.

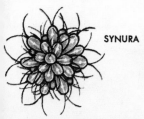

SYNURA

ZYGNEMA

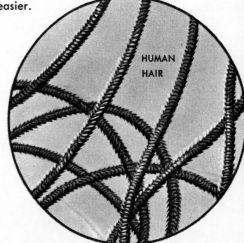

HUMAN HAIR

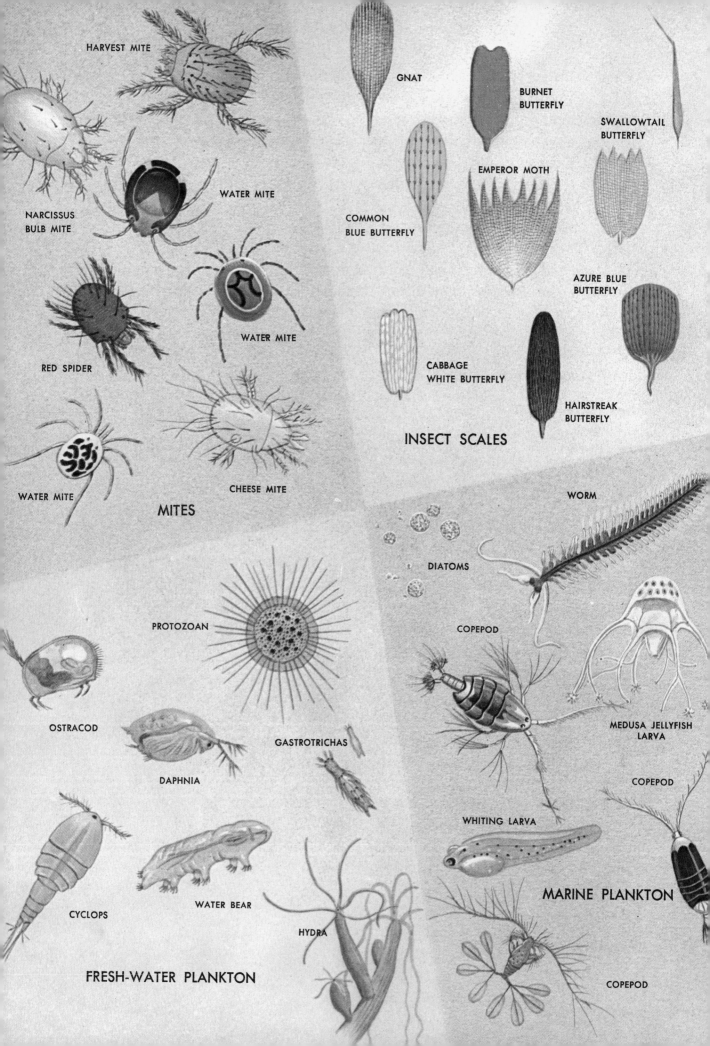

HARVEST MITE

WATER MITE

NARCISSUS
BULB MITE

RED SPIDER

WATER MITE

WATER MITE

CHEESE MITE

MITES

GNAT

BURNET
BUTTERFLY

SWALLOWTAIL
BUTTERFLY

EMPEROR MOTH

COMMON
BLUE BUTTERFLY

AZURE BLUE
BUTTERFLY

CABBAGE
WHITE BUTTERFLY

HAIRSTREAK
BUTTERFLY

INSECT SCALES

WORM

DIATOMS

PROTOZOAN

COPEPOD

OSTRACOD

MEDUSA JELLYFISH
LARVA

DAPHNIA

GASTROTRICHAS

COPEPOD

WHITING LARVA

CYCLOPS

WATER BEAR

MARINE PLANKTON

HYDRA

FRESH-WATER PLANKTON

COPEPOD

When focusing, you must *always* keep

How do you focus it? in mind this rule: *Never focus downward. Always focus upward*. If you focus downward, you will surely, sooner or later, push the front of the objective through the slide. This will not only break the slide, and perhaps ruin a valuable specimen, but it may also break the front lens of the objective. Mindful of this, turn slowly the coarse adjustment toward yourself, so that the tube rises from the slide. When the hair comes clearly into view, change from the coarse adjustment to the fine one. Although you must turn the coarse adjustment only in one direction when focusing, you may turn the fine adjustment in either direction, *as long as you do not turn it more than half a turn*. Thus, with the fine adjustment, you can bring the hair into clear focus. You will probably find that you have to adjust the mirror again.

After you have studied the hair for a while, you may want to magnify it more. If the microscope has only one nosepiece, raise the objective far above the slide, unscrew the objective to take it out of the nosepiece, and then put another, higher-power, objective into the nosepiece. Then focus in the same way as you did when using the low-power objective.

Illustrated on the left are other specimens which may be viewed under the microscope. Mites belong to a family of tiny animals related to spiders and scorpions. They often infest other animals, including humans, plants, and foods. Protozoa, along with other tiny animals, as well as plants, make up the plankton, which floats on the surface of oceans and lakes. Plankton serves as the food for many forms of sea life.

If the microscope has a nosepiece with two objectives, simply turn the lower part of the nosepiece around so that the other objective is in line with the tube. If the microscope is well made, changing the objective should not change the focus very much. However, some focusing with the fine adjustment will probably be necessary. Also, you will have to adjust the lighting again.

If the microscope has a third objective, move it into place just as you did the second one. However, you cannot use this objective simply by focusing. This objective, usually the one marked 97x, is an *oil immersion lens*. It has this name because to use it, you usually put the foremost lens of the objective into a drop of oil placed upon the cover glass. Again you will have to focus, and this time be very careful, because the front of the objective is nearly touching the cover glass. The oil you use must be *cedarwood oil*. This oil can be obtained from microscope dealers.

After examining the hair, you will have to clean the equipment.

How do you clean the equipment? Turn the coarse adjustment knob to raise the oil immersion lens from the slide. Then wet a special kind of tissue, called *lens tissue,* in a liquid called *xylol*. With the wetted tissue, wipe all the oil off the oil immersion lens. It is well to use two separate pieces of tissue for two wipings. The xylol evaporates quickly, but may leave a foggy deposit on the lens, so wipe the lens with a dry piece of lens tissue.

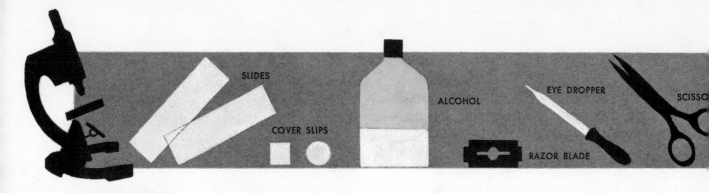

SLIDES
COVER SLIPS
ALCOHOL
EYE DROPPER
RAZOR BLADE
SCISSO

If you wish to keep the slide with the mounted hair, wipe off with xylol any excess balsam that has oozed out from under the cover glass, label the slide, and store it. If, on the other hand, you do not wish to keep the slide mount, place a drop or two of xylol around the edges of the cover glass. This will work its way under the glass and dissolve the balsam so that you can remove the cover glass. Now all you have to do is wipe the cover glass and the slide with some xylol or lens tissue.

If you want to make microscopy your hobby, you will

What equipment will you need to become a microscopist?

have to start with certain basic equipment: a microscope; glass slides (at least a dozen to begin with); cover glasses (about two dozen, since these break very easily); tweezers (or forceps); a medicine dropper; a probe (made by sticking the eye-end of a needle into an eraser removed from a pencil); a sharp knife, or single-edge razor blade; sharp-pointed scissors; Canada balsam (or fingernail polish); and xylol (or acetone). While a simple microscope will reveal many wonders of the world around you, this instrument has its limits. You cannot buy one that will give the 300x power of van Leeuwenhoek's. Even a good simple

microscope will not magnify more than 10x, and the very best will magnify only 20x. In order to really do interesting work in microscopy, you need a compound microscope.

A laboratory, or biological, compound microscope is a

What kind of microscope should you get?

very expensive instrument that costs several hundred dollars. However, it is possible to purchase a so-called *amateur microscope* which is much less expensive. This is a smaller model of the laboratory microscope. It lacks some refinements that only a highly-trained scientist would need for his work, but in your microscopy, you will not miss them at all. These amateur microscopes are not toys — they are real compound microscopes that will produce a clear image magnified 300 to 500 times. You can buy such a microscope for $11 to $20. This may seem like quite a lot of money, but if you begin immediately to put away nickels and dimes that you find you really do not have to spend, you will have saved up the needed money sooner than now seems likely. When you are ready to buy your microscope, you will be wise to consult a science teacher in your school. He can give you advice on how to go about buying the microscope. One good place to buy an amateur mi-

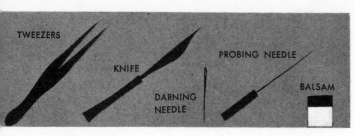

TWEEZERS

KNIFE

PROBING NEEDLE

DARNING NEEDLE

BALSAM

SNOW CRYSTALS MAGNIFIED

croscope is from a mail-order house. Consult its catalog carefully before you order. Make sure there is a guarantee that the microscope will be replaced if it is defective when you get it.

The World of Invisible Life — Bacteria and Protozoa

What are the smallest plants in the world?

All around us are billions of tiny living things that are too small to be seen with the unaided eyes. Among the smallest of these living things are plants called *bacteria*. A single one of these plants is a *bacterium*. Some bacteria are so small that 10,000 of them could be placed on the period at the end of this sentence.

Each bacterium is a single living cell. This means that it is a separate bit of living matter that can live and grow by itself. It can take into itself food and oxygen. It uses the food for nourishment, and the oxygen to help it nourish itself, grow and move.

Where are bacteria found?

Bacteria may be found all around us — in the earth, in water and in the air. There are millions of bacteria on your skin, in your mouth, your nasal passages, and elsewhere inside your body. There are thousands of different kinds of bacteria. They are man's invisible friends and foes. They are both useful and harmful to man.

How are bacteria useful?

Among the useful bacteria are those that produce buttermilk and vinegar, age cheese, and help in the curing of leather. Probably the most valuable service that bacteria give to

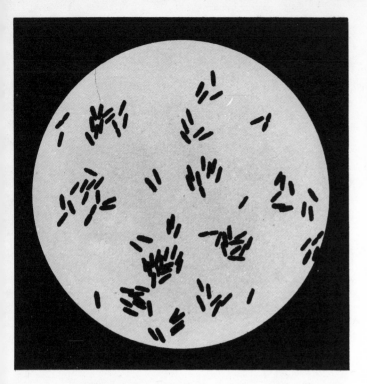

Bacilli, rod-shaped bacteria, may be useful or harmful.

and forth rapidly and push the bacterium through the liquid. Some bacteria have cilia growing out from all parts of the cell wall. Others have just a single thread at one or both ends. Still others have a tuft of cilia at one end.

When do they thrive best? Since bacteria are so important to man, it is useful to know in what conditions bacteria live and grow. Most bacteria thrive best at the temperature of the human body — a little

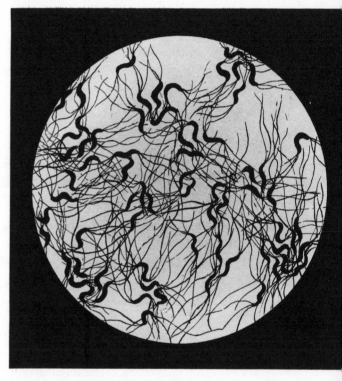

Some spirilla, spiral bacteria, have thread-like ends.

man is to cause decay. If decay bacteria were not constantly at work, the earth would become littered with the dead bodies of animals and plants.

Harmful bacteria are those that cause disease in animals and plants. Among the diseases caused in man by bacteria are pneumonia, typhoid fever and tuberculosis. Fortunately, there are more harmless bacteria than harmful ones.

What do bacteria look like? Bacteria may have any one of three shapes. Some are round like a ball. A bacterium of this shape is called a *coccus*. Another kind of bacterium is shaped like a rod, and is called a *bacillus*. The third kind of bacterium has a spiral shape, and is called a *spirillum*.

Some bacteria can move when they are in a liquid. A bacterium of this kind has extremely thin threads of living matter growing out from its cell wall. These threads, called *cilia*, lash back

less than 99 degrees Fahrenheit. Both lower and higher temperatures slow the growth of bacteria. Freezing and boiling will kill most bacteria. You can now see that putting food in the refrigerator slows the growth of bacteria that may be on the food, and thereby prevents the food from becoming spoiled. Also,

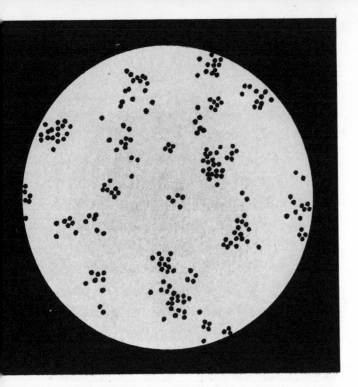

Cocci are ball-like, or spherically-shaped, bacteria.

Bacteria reproduce themselves very rapidly. It takes only about thirty minutes for one bacterium to become two. If all the offspring of one bacterium could go on reproducing for twelve hours, there would be seventeen million of them. If this process continued for five days, bacteria would fill all the oceans to a depth of one mile. Of course, nothing like this can take place, because most bacteria do not find the nourishment or favor-

How fast do bacteria reproduce?

cooking food not only makes it easier and tastier to eat, but also kills harmful bacteria that may be on it.

Bacteria need much moisture in order to thrive. Thus, if we keep food dry, we keep it from spoiling by the growth of bacteria upon it. Darkness is another condition in which bacteria thrive. A strong light will slow the growth of bacteria or kill them. Now you can see why a sunny room is a healthy room.

In most civilized countries, the law requires that bacteria in milk be killed by raising the temperature of the milk to 145 degrees Fahrenheit and keeping it at this temperature for thirty minutes. This process for killing bacteria is called *pasteurization* and was discovered by the great French bacteriologist Louis Pasteur. A bacteriologist is a scientist who studies and works with bacteria — or the science of bacteriology.

What is the process of pasteurization?

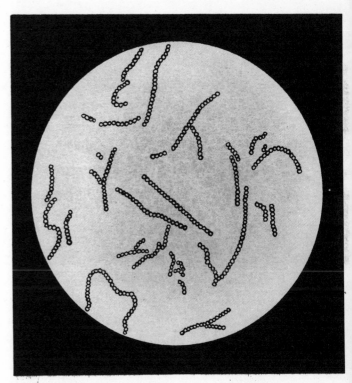

Cocci may also grow in pairs, clusters or in chains.

able conditions in which to grow and reproduce.

One of the best ways to get harmless bacteria is to make a *hay infusion*. Fill a two-quart glass jar almost full of water. If you can get water

How can you get bacteria?

9:00 A.M.

9:20 A.M.

9:40 A.M.

10:00 A.M.

Many bacteria reproduce by splitting in two — a half hour process. Some split in 20 min.

from a stream or lake, you can proceed immediately with the rest of the experiment. If you take water from a tap, allow the jar to stand uncovered for three days, so that excess oxygen that is probably dissolved in the water may escape. Paste a label on the outside of the jar at the level of the surface of the water, so that you may add more water to the jar, if needed. Add only water that you have allowed to stand for a while, like the original jar.

Cut a handful of hay or dry grass into short lengths and put it into the water in the jar. Cover the jar and place it where daylight, but not direct sunlight, will reach it. In about three or four days, you will notice a scum on the surface of the water and an accompanying unpleasant odor. The scum is formed by billions of bacteria.

Plunge the tip of your medicine dropper beneath the scum, and draw up some clear water. Place a drop of this water on a glass slide. Using your probe, pick up a very small amount of scum — just enough to cover the point of the needle — and dip the needle into the drop of water on the slide. Place a cover glass over the drop. Focus

How do you prepare bacteria for the microscope?

carefully and adjust the mirror in several different positions as you seek for bacteria in the field of your microscope. If you see nothing but a blurry blob of material, it means that you have placed too large an amount of scum on the slide. Make a new slide, using only one-tenth as much scum. In trying to find bacteria, the lighting is very important. Spend considerable time in manipulating the mirror. In your report, describe the shapes of the bacteria you see.

There are many other sources of bacteria among everyday things. Imitate Leeuwenhoek by scraping with a tooth-

An organism continues to reproduce in a new culture.

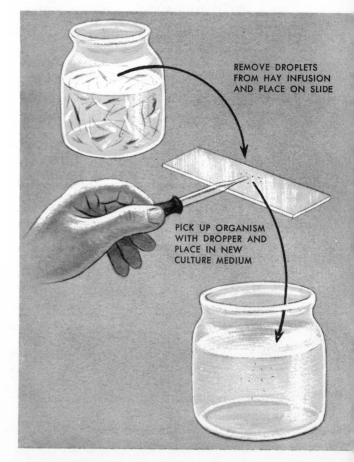

REMOVE DROPLETS FROM HAY INFUSION AND PLACE ON SLIDE

PICK UP ORGANISM WITH DROPPER AND PLACE IN NEW CULTURE MEDIUM

(1) *Streptococci.* (2) *Staphylocci.* (3) *Tetanus bacilli.* (4) *Typhoid bacilli.* (5) *Tuberculosis bacilli.* (6) *Cholera vibrio.* All are disease-causing bacteria in man.

pick a tiny bit of the white material from your teeth, just at the gum-line. Place this white material in a drop of water, on a slide. Make a few cuts in a peach or an apple, and let the fruit stand in a warm, damp place for a few days. Place a bit of the material from the cut in a drop of water on a slide, and examine it for bacteria. Mix a pinch of soil in a little water. Place a drop of this mixture on a slide and examine it for bacteria.

Placing bacteria in a drop of water on a slide makes a preparation that requires much manipulation of the mirror in order to be able to see the bacteria at all. This method has the advantage of presenting for examination live bacteria, some of which may be moving. There is, however, another method of preparing bacteria that makes them much easier to see.

You can prepare a slide of bacteria so that they will be easily seen, if you *stain* the bacteria either red or blue. First, of course, you will need the stain. The blue stain is called *methylene blue,* and the red stain is *eosin.* You can buy both of them from a pharmacist. They are cheap, and you need very little of each. If you buy the stains in dry form, dissolve in half a tumblerful of water just as much of either as you can pick up on the end of a knife blade. This will give you enough to last for months. It is wise to keep the stains in stoppered bottles, so that the water does not evaporate.

How can you stain bacteria?

Many microorganisms flourish in a hay infusion. Shown are the *colpoda, hay bacillus,* and *volvox,* all magnified.

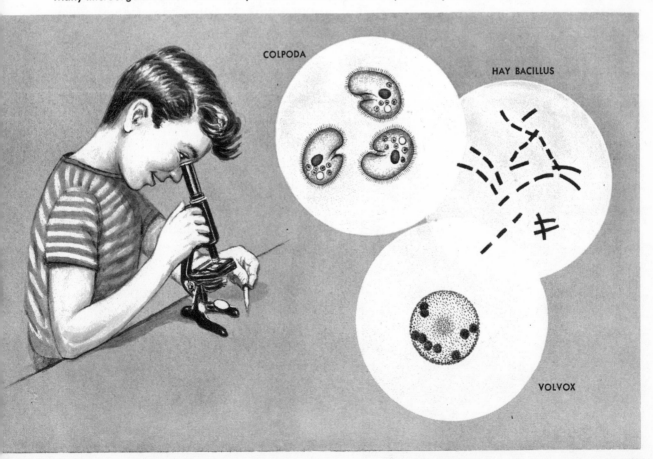

COLPODA

HAY BACILLUS

VOLVOX

If you cannot buy these two stains, you can use ink. For the blue stain use the "permanent" kind of blue fountain pen ink, which contains methylene blue. For red stain use any kind of red ink.

Prepare the stained slide in this manner:

How can you prepare a stained slide?

Place a drop of water on a clean slide. Using your probe, add a small amount of the bacteria-containing material to the wa-ter, and spread the mixture into a broad smear. Grasp the slide by the edges near one end, and hold it several inches above a candle flame until the water evaporates. Hold the slide sufficiently high above the flame so that the water does not boil. You do not want to cook the bacteria.

When all of the water has evaporated and the slide is thoroughly dry, pass the slide through the candle flame rapidly three or four times. This action is called *fixing* the smear.

When the slide has cooled thoroughly, drop a stain from your medicine dropper on the fixed smear. Some bacteria stain better with blue dye and others stain better with red dye. You will have to experiment with both colors to see which one best stains the kind of bacteria you are working with.

Leave the stain on the smear for about a minute. Some bacteria will need more than a minute to stain thoroughly. Again, you will have to learn this by experience. After the stain has been on the smear for the proper length of time, wash it off with running tap water. Then, place the slide, smear-side up, on a paper towel. Fold the towel over and blot the slide carefully. Do not rub the towel on the smear. This will destroy the smear. Now, examine the slide under the microscope.

There is another way to prepare a slide of bacteria, so that you can observe them alive. This is called the *hanging drop* method. There is a kind of thick glass slide that

What is a hanging drop mount?

Picture-instructions for preparing a stained slide:

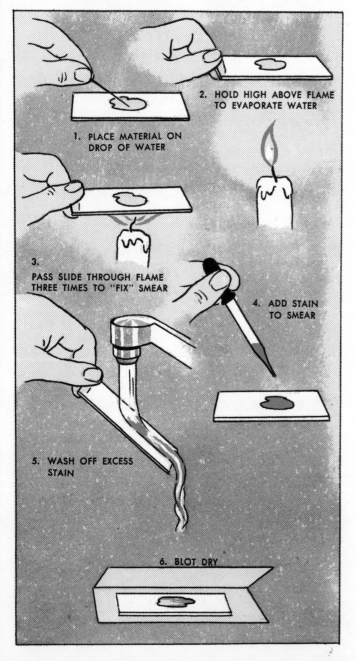

1. PLACE MATERIAL ON DROP OF WATER

2. HOLD HIGH ABOVE FLAME TO EVAPORATE WATER

3. PASS SLIDE THROUGH FLAME THREE TIMES TO "FIX" SMEAR

4. ADD STAIN TO SMEAR

5. WASH OFF EXCESS STAIN

6. BLOT DRY

has a little well ground into its center. This slide is used to set up a hanging drop mount. Such slides are expensive, so you would probably do best if you make your own hanging drop apparatus.

How can you make your own hanging drop mount? Cut a piece of cardboard exactly the size of a glass slide. You can do this best by tracing the outline of the slide on the cardboard. Now, cut the cardboard into three equal lengths. With your pointed scissors, cut a hole, no bigger than half an inch, in the center of each of the three pieces of cardboard. Glue the three pieces together, one on top of the other, so that there is a single hole through all three. Cement this cardboard "washer" to the center of a glass slide. Cover one of your fingers lightly with petroleum jelly — like Vaseline. Holding a cover glass in your hand, scrape the jelly off your finger, using all the edges of the cover glass, until there is a rim of jelly all around the edges of the cover glass. Place the glass on the table, jelly-side up. Using your probe, place a mixture of water and a drop of the bacteria-containing material you want to examine on the center of the cover glass.

Hold the glass slide so that the cardboard washer is underneath and the hole in the washer is right over the center of the cover glass. Lower the slide, and press the washer firmly on the jelly rim of the cover glass. Then, with a quick motion, turn the slide over. A drop of the mixture you are to examine

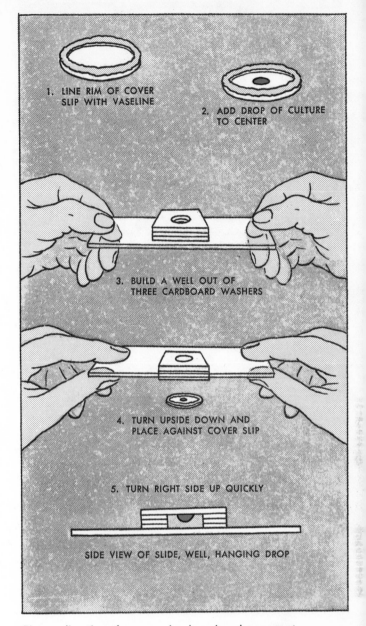

1. LINE RIM OF COVER SLIP WITH VASELINE

2. ADD DROP OF CULTURE TO CENTER

3. BUILD A WELL OUT OF THREE CARDBOARD WASHERS

4. TURN UPSIDE DOWN AND PLACE AGAINST COVER SLIP

5. TURN RIGHT SIDE UP QUICKLY

SIDE VIEW OF SLIDE, WELL, HANGING DROP

Picture-directions for preparing hanging drop mount.

will be hanging down from the cover glass. Examine the drop under the microscope, focusing it carefully.

What are the smallest animals in the world? Perhaps, when you were looking at bacteria from your hay infusion, you saw a large object swim across your field of view. This large object was a one-celled animal of the kind called *protozoa*. This name means "earliest

easier to find protozoa and a little harder to find bacteria. Also, the amount of scum seemed to lessen. This was because the protozoa were feeding on the bacteria. They increased in number as they ate up the bacteria.

Protozoa are interesting to watch under a microscope because they have so many different forms and they move about in many different ways. You can see them hunting and catching their food, which is usually bacteria, but may

Stagnant water may teem with harmful bacteria and protozoa.

ENTAMOEBA HISTOLYTICA

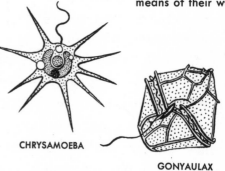

Flagellated protozoa swim by means of their whips.

CHRYSAMOEBA

GONYAULAX

EUGLENA

form of animals" and refers to the fact that protozoa were probably the first animals to appear in the oceans of the earth hundreds of millions of years ago. They are still water animals, and are found in the seas, lakes and streams. A single one of these animals is called a *protozoan*.

A protozoan, like a bacterium, is a separate bit of living matter that can take in and use food, get rid of wastes, move, grow and reproduce. There are thousands of kinds. Most are harmless, but a few are harmful to man. Among the harmful ones are those that cause such diseases as malaria, dysentery and sleeping sickness.

What do the protozoa eat? If you worked with your hay infusion for several days, you may have noticed that it became continually

be just bits of once-living plant or animal material floating about in the water — or it may be other protozoa.

How can you examine protozoa? The hanging drop method is one of the best ways of preparing a slide for the examination of protozoa. The main difficulty with this method is that the drop provides the tiny animals with such a large ocean to swim in that they swim either above or below the level on which your microscope is focused. One big advantage of the hanging drop mount for protozoa is that the water does not evaporate easily, and you can watch the tiny animals for a long time.

Another way to prepare a slide for the observation of protozoa is simply to place a drop of water from a hay infusion on a glass slide and cover it gently with a cover glass. When obtaining the drop, poke your medicine dropper beneath the scum on the surface of the infusion.

The cover glass flattens the drop of water so much that there is very little room for the protozoa to swim up and down. Once you have focused on one of them, it will usually remain in focus for a long time. The main disadvantage of this method of mounting is that the water evaporates quite rapidly. While you are looking at a particularly interesting protozoan, the slide may dry up right under your eyes. You can prevent this from happening by putting a rim of petroleum jelly around the edges of

Ciliated protozoa swim by means of hair-like organs.

STENTOR

DIDIDIUM

STYLONICHIA

the cover glass, *after* it is placed upon the drop of water.

You will find that many protozoa are

How can you keep protozoa in place?

simply too active to enable you to get a good look at them, especially when you are using the high-power objective.

One way to keep the protozoa in place is to trap them in the fibers of a piece of thread. Fray a half-inch piece of thread so that the fibers make a mat. Flatten this mat, and place it in the drop of water on the slide, before you put on the cover glass. The fibers will form a "net" that will entangle and hold, or slow down, the protozoa in the water.

You may see one or more protozoa

How do protozoa move about?

move around under your microscope, and, unless you know just what to look for, you

may be unable to tell just how they move. Some protozoa move through the water by means of cilia along the sides of their bodies. Some protozoans have at one end a thread of living matter that is longer and thicker than a cilium. This thread is called a *flagellum*, a Latin

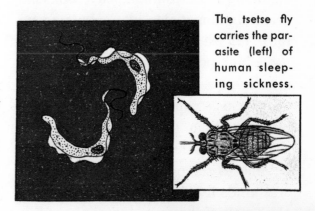

The tsetse fly carries the parasite (left) of human sleeping sickness.

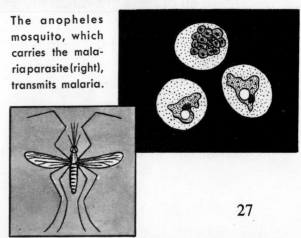

The anopheles mosquito, which carries the malaria parasite (right), transmits malaria.

27

word that means "whip." Some protozoa pull themselves through the water by beating these whips down to their sides. Others use the whip as a tail and push themselves through the water in the same way you can push a small boat along by moving a single oar back and forth in the water behind the boat's stern.

The only whip-bearing protozoan that **What is a Peranema?** you are likely to find in a hay infusion is one called *Peranema*. You will recognize this one because it has two whips, a long one and a short one, at opposite ends of the body. You may be puzzled to understand what makes *Peranema* move, when its whips seem to be standing still. If you look closely at the tip of the long one, you will see that it is vibrating back and forth very rapidly. Also, *Peranema* is always changing shape. Sometimes it looks like a radish, sometimes like a bulging potato. To see *Peranema* well, you must use a high-power objective and a rather dim light.

If you scrape the inside of your mouth with a toothpick and make a slide of the material obtained, you may be able to see other whip-bearers. Several kinds live in the human body, and almost all of them are entirely harmless.

Your hay infusion may yield a more or **What is an amoeba?** less shapeless protozoan called an *amoeba*. This protozoan has no particular shape. Sometimes it may be nearly round, and at other times it may have a half dozen ragged projections sticking out from the central mass of its body.

You must watch an amoeba for some **How does an amoeba move?** time in order to see how it moves. In the first place, it spends a great part of its time resting, or, at least, not moving. Secondly, an amoeba moves very slowly. As you watch, you will see that a projection of living material slowly moves outward from the main part of its body. This projection is called a *pseudopod,* or false foot. Then, you will see more living material streaming into the false foot, which will grow larger. Eventually, all of the amoeba will have streamed into what was a pseudopod, and the whole amoeba will now be at the place to which the pseudopod first reached out.

One of the most common kind of protozoa is a *paramecium*. **What is a paramecium?** It is shaped something like a long slipper. Its body is covered with cilia that beat back and forth very rapidly. Since there are hundreds of cilia on the body, and all are acting like tiny oars, the paramecium is moved through the water very rapidly. A paramecium is also one of the largest of the protozoa. It may reach a diameter of more than 1/100 of an inch. If you see one under your microscope, it might be interesting to remove the slide from the clips and see whether you can see the paramecium with your naked eye. To do this place the slide on a black background, and shine a light directly down upon the cover glass. The paramecia will be seen as bright moving specks.

Protozoa, such as the amoeba and paramecia, are large enough so that we not only can study their general form, but we can examine what is inside them.

What is inside a protozoan?

Since each protozoan is a single living cell, it possesses some of the characteristics of all living cells. It is surrounded by a membrane that holds it together. The living material that is within the cell membrane is called *cytoplasm*. If you examine the cytoplasm carefully, you will see that it looks grainy, as if it were made up of grains of colorless sand. It is this graininess that enables the cytoplasm in the amoeba to stream into its false feet, just as sand in a sack can be made to flow around by moving the sack.

Within the cytoplasm is a large dark dot. This is the cell's *nucleus*. All the movements and activities of the protozoan are directed by it. It is somewhat as though the nucleus were the cell's brain.

Somewhere in the cytoplasm of an amoeba or a paramecium, you will see one or two (or more) large clear circles. In the paramecium, you may

How do protozoa collect wastes and water?

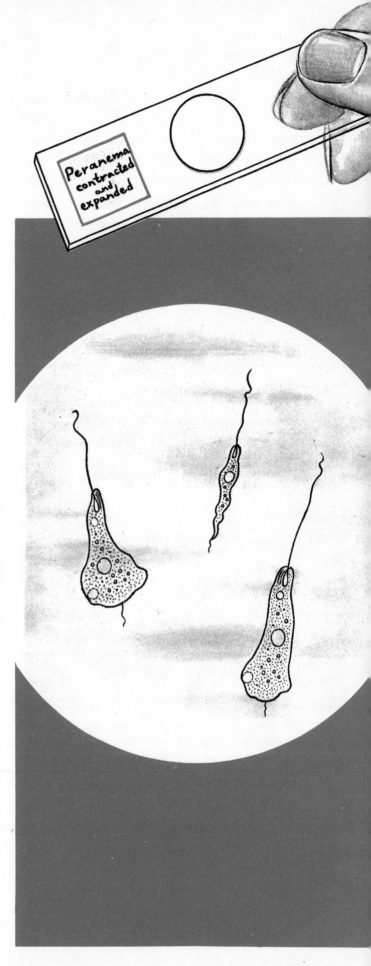

Peranema changes shape by contracting, expanding.

see a clear, star-shaped spot. These are *contractile vacuoles*. They move about within the cytoplasm collecting waste materials and excess water. When they reach the membrane of the protozoan, they suddenly contract and expel their burden outside the cell wall. After this happens, the vacuole becomes very small, but as it moves about picking up waste materials and water, it grows larger.

Also within the cytoplasm, you will

How does the amoeba eat? probably see small dark dots with lighter circles around them. These are bits of food that the proto-

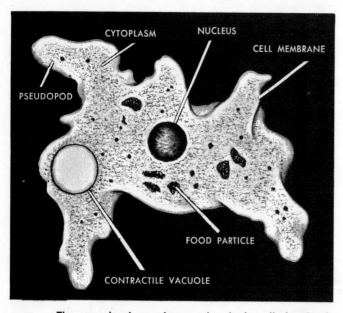

CYTOPLASM NUCLEUS
CELL MEMBRANE
PSEUDOPOD
FOOD PARTICLE
CONTRACTILE VACUOLE

The amoeba is a microscopic, single-celled animal. Its name comes from the Greek word for *change.*

zoan has taken into itself, and it is interesting to watch how this is done. When an amoeba comes upon a bit of food, it reaches out two pseudopods to surround the food particle. When the pseudopods have curved completely around the piece of food, they meet. Then the

membrane between them dissolves, and the food particle is inside the amoeba.

A paramecium has a tougher cell mem-

How does a paramecium get its food? brane, and cannot, therefore, put out pseudopods to surround a bit of food. Instead, the paramecium has a mouth and a gullet into which nourishment is taken. If you look closely at a paramecium, you will see a groove along one side, near the front end. This is the *oral groove*. Focus very carefully, and you may be able to see that the oral groove is lined with cilia. When a paramecium comes upon food particles, usually bacteria, the beating of the cilia shove the particles along the oral groove to a point near the middle of the body where there is a tube. The opening of this tube is the *mouth,* and the tube, itself, is the *gullet.* When food particles reach the lower end of the gullet, they collect into a ball, and this ball, along with a little water, floats into the cytoplasm. You see the food as a dark dot, and the water as the light circle around the dot. Together, they make up a *food vacuole.*

Since the feeding actions of protozoa

How can you feed protozoa? are so interesting, you may want to provide food in order to watch them take it into their bodies. Pick off from a cake of yeast a piece about the size of the eye of a needle. Mash the speck of yeast in a drop of water. Place a little of this mixture in the center of a drop of water that contains protozoa. Place a cover slip on the

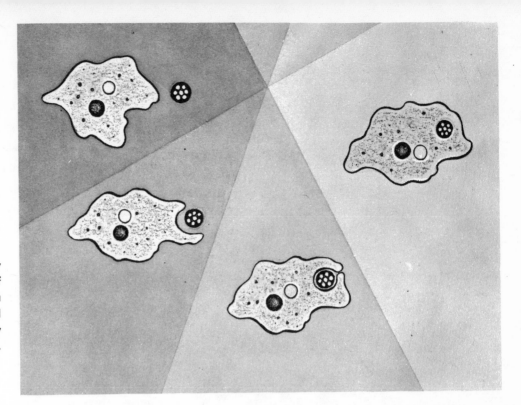

The illustrations show how the pseudopods of an amoeba engulf a particle of food, until the food is completely inside the protozoan.

water. Dip the end of a toothpick into red ink and transfer a small drop of ink to the edge of the cover glass. The red dye in the ink will make it easier for you to see the food-taking activities.

When bacteria or protozoa find themselves in conditions that are too dry, they temporarily suspend their living processes, without actually dying. To accomplish this, they surround themselves with a very tough covering that protects them from completely drying out, and also from sudden changes in temperature. A bacteria in this condition is called a *spore,* and a protozoan is a *cyst.* Spores and cysts are very light and can be easily carried by even the lightest breezes.

How do bacteria and protozoa suspend life?

When a spore or cyst again happens upon wet conditions, the thick covering dissolves and the bacterium or the protozoan goes on living just as it did before it encountered unfavorable conditions.

Since the grass you used for making a hay infusion was dry, you may wonder where water-living creatures like bacteria and protozoa came from after the grass had soaked for a few days. Bacteria and protozoa that had been living on the hay-infusion grass before it dried formed spores and cysts when drying took place. When you placed the grass in water, the walls of the spores and cysts dissolved.

Where do hay-infusion bacteria and protozoa come from?

A few days after you put the dry grass into the water, a scum made up of bacteria appeared in your hay infusion. For a few days, the amount of scum increased, thereby

How do the number of bacteria and protozoa increase?

showing that the number of bacteria was increasing. If you examined the water every day, you found that at first there were few protozoa, and then their number increased. Since the number of bacteria and protozoa *increased,* they could not all have been on the grass as spores or cysts. Where did the new ones come from? The bacteria and protozoa reproduced themselves — processes which are very interesting to watch.

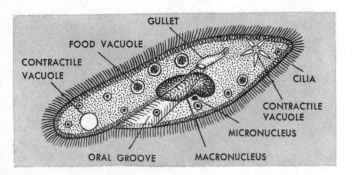

The paramecium swims by means of cilia. It reproduces by splitting or cell division.

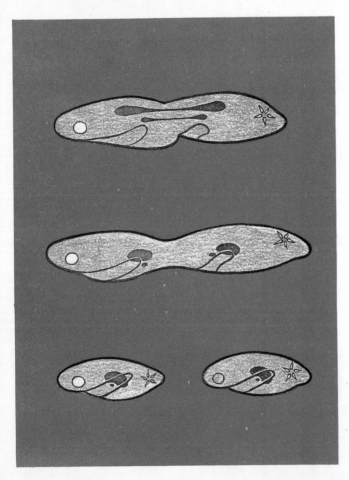

When a bacterium or protozoan begins to reproduce, its nucleus lengthens, narrows in the middle, pinches off to become two nuclei, and then each new nucleus moves to opposite ends of the cell. While the nucleus is going through its splitting process, the whole cell begins to do the same. It lengthens, narrows in the middle, and finally pinches in two. This process lags just a little behind that of the nucleus. The splitting process is called *cell division.* The reproduction of a bacterium takes just about half an hour. This means that you can easily watch the whole process without tiring. The cell division of a protozoan may take longer, but not so long that you cannot watch it.

One of the convenient things about the cell division of a protozoan is that during this process, the little animal hardly moves about. Thus, it is easy to see beneath a microscope. To find a reproducing bacterium or protozoan you must search around carefully on your slide. Move the slide back and forth beneath the microscope's objective. As you have probably already learned, when you move the slide to the right, it seems to move to the left when you look through the microscope. And, of course, when you move the slide to the left, it seems to move to the right. This is confusing, but with a little practice, you can learn to manipulate the slide correctly.

As you watch the process of cell division, continually focus up and down with the fine adjustment on your micro-

How do they reproduce?

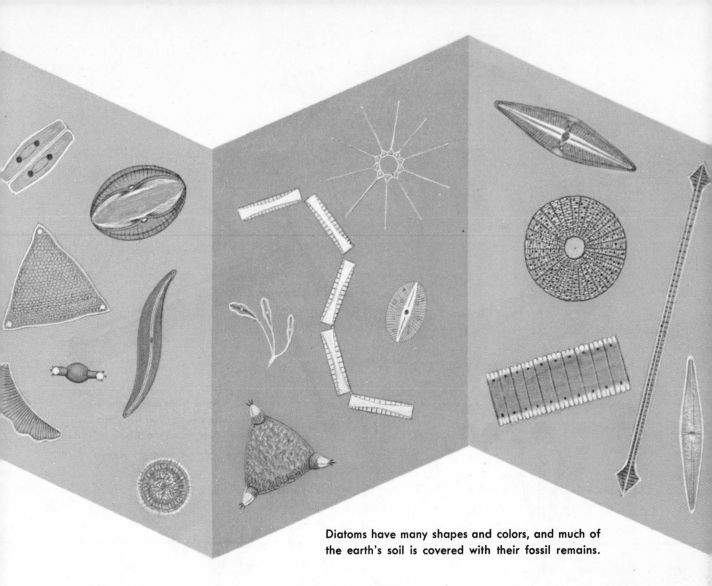

Diatoms have many shapes and colors, and much of the earth's soil is covered with their fossil remains.

scope. By doing this, you may be able to see that other small objects within the cell, besides the nucleus, split and move to opposite ends of the cell. A small drop of red dye or ink will help you to see this part of cell division.

One-celled plants, called *diatoms*, are able to use certain chemicals dissolved in water to build either a shell or a framework of hard glassy material around their soft bodies. Diatoms live in the waters of streams and lakes, oceans and in damp soil. When they die, their tiny glasslike

What kind of microscopic plants live in "houses"?

houses settle to the bottom of the water. Sometimes these little plants live in such great numbers that their tiny shells cover the bottom of bodies of water in thick layers. If the stream or the lake dries up, the layers of diatom shells form a kind of hard earth called *diatomaceous earth*.

If you live near a body of water, you may be able to get specimens of diatoms to examine under your microscope. In streams and lakes, your best chance of finding diatoms is in the mud at the bottom of the water. Take a sample of this mud mixed with water and make microscopic slides from it. Any sample of ocean water may contain diatoms.

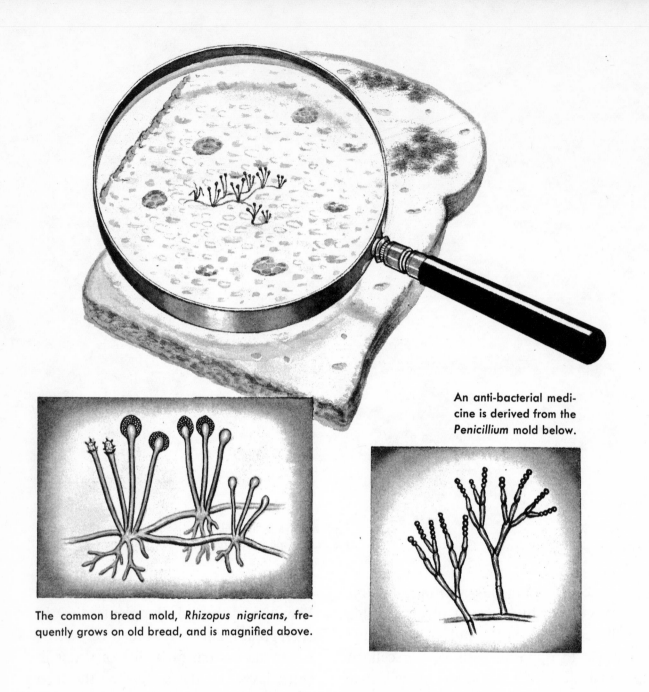

An anti-bacterial medicine is derived from the *Penicillium* mold below.

The common bread mold, *Rhizopus nigricans*, frequently grows on old bread, and is magnified above.

Molds, Mildew, Yeast Budding

Sprinkle water on four or five slices of bread. Wipe the damp side of these slices across the floor, taking care not to crumble the bread. Put the

How can you grow plants on a slice of bread?

bread into a closet or some other warm, dark place. Two days later, examine the slices. You will probably find on them patches of a white cottony material peppered with black dots. This material is the thick growth of a plant called *common bread mold*.

To examine this mold, place a small piece of bread on the stage of your microscope. Shine a bright light down on the mold. Be sure that the light does not also shine in your eyes and hinder your viewing. Use the low-power objective to examine the bread mold.

Note that the white cottony material is

What do molds look like?

a tangled mass of filaments. This is called a *mycelium.* The threadlike growths are made of living matter. Trace one of the filaments. You will see that it runs horizontally for a short distance, then it branches into several vertical filaments. On the top of each of these vertical growths is a black knob. These are *sporangia,* or *spore cases.* Within each one of these cases are a large number of spores. Sooner or later, the knobs will burst open. The spores are so light that they will easily float away in the air. When a spore alights on some material that the mold can use for food, the spore will grow into a whole new mold plant. It was spores wiped up from the floor that grew into mold on your bread.

Directly beneath the vertical filaments are others that branch downward into the bread. These filaments act like roots by obtaining from the bread the nourishment the mold plant needs in order to live and grow.

Most molds are harmless to man, though

How are molds useful to man?

a few may cause diseases. One such disease is "athlete's foot." Some molds are useful, such as the ones which give flavor to certain kinds of cheese. By far the most important use of molds is to provide the basis for the drugs called *antibiotics.* These drugs have helped to conquer certain diseases that took thousands of lives before antibiotics were discovered. Some antibiotics are penicillin, streptomycin, and aureomycin.

Having examined the mold on the bread by means of the low-power objective, examine it in a different way. Scrape some mold off the bread and place it on a glass slide. Add a drop of water and a drop of alcohol. Then cover it with a cover glass. Light the slide in the usual way; that is, by means of light reflected upward from the microscope mirror. First examine the mold with the low-power objective. Then use the high-power objective. You will see that each mold plant is made of many cells. You might even be able to see a nucleus in one of these cells.

It is possible that along with, or instead of, common bread mold, you will find an orange, black, green, or pink mold growing on your bread. Each color represents a different species of mold. Examine each one and make a comparison of the shapes and colors of the different parts of each mold.

Have you ever seen a whitish, powdery

What is mildew?

material on shoes or leather jackets that were stored in a damp place? Or, perhaps, during a damp summer, you have seen the same kind of whitish spots on curtains or fabric furniture coverings. Or, you may have seen black streaks on sheets or pillow cases that your mother stored while they were still damp. Both the white spots and the black streaks were caused by *mildew,* which is the general name for a group of plants very much like true molds. Mildews have a mycelium and sporangia. Mildews not only stain and rot leather and cloth, but they also destroy many useful plants, among them roses,

SPORE CASE OF BREAD MOLD

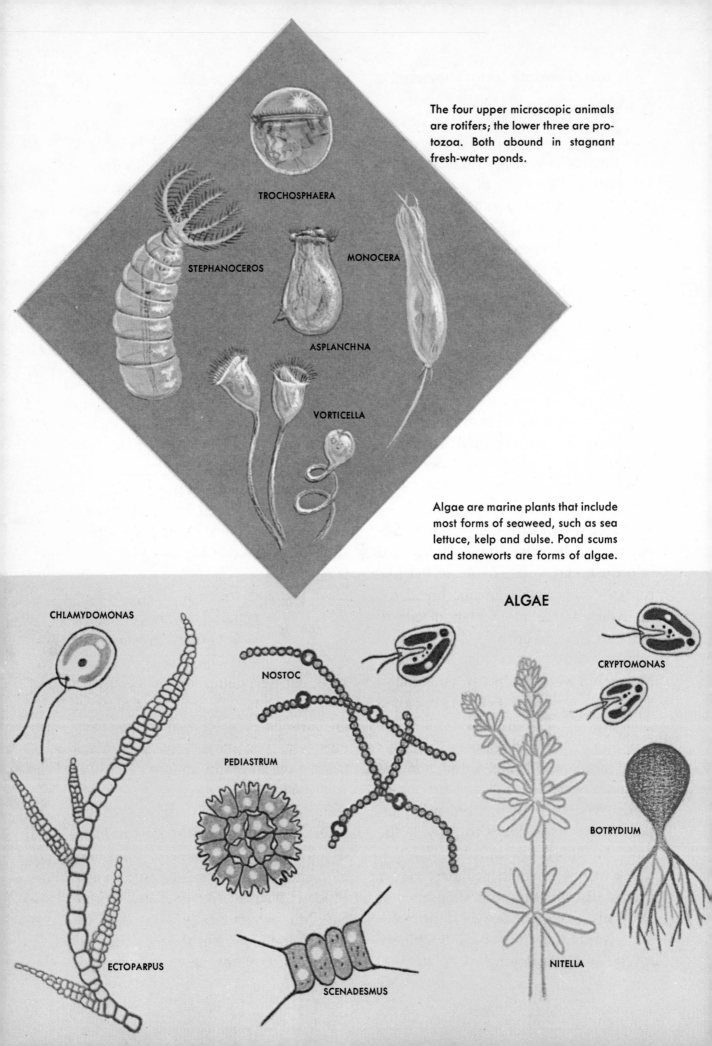

The four upper microscopic animals are rotifers; the lower three are protozoa. Both abound in stagnant fresh-water ponds.

TROCHOSPHAERA

STEPHANOCEROS

MONOCERA

ASPLANCHNA

VORTICELLA

Algae are marine plants that include most forms of seaweed, such as sea lettuce, kelp and dulse. Pond scums and stoneworts are forms of algae.

ALGAE

CHLAMYDOMONAS

NOSTOC

CRYPTOMONAS

PEDIASTRUM

BOTRYDIUM

ECTOPARPUS

SCENADESMUS

NITELLA

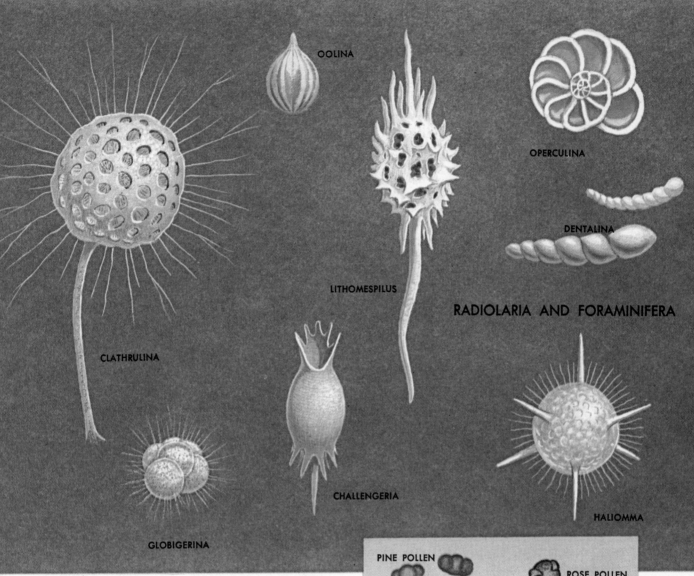

OOLINA

OPERCULINA

DENTALINA

LITHOMESPILUS

RADIOLARIA AND FORAMINIFERA

CLATHRULINA

CHALLENGERIA

HALIOMMA

GLOBIGERINA

Both *Radiolaria* and *Foraminifera* are shelled protozoa that live in the sea. Radiolaria have delicate glass-like shells. Foraminifera have chalk-like shells.

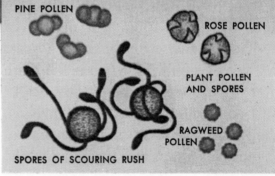

PINE POLLEN

ROSE POLLEN

PLANT POLLEN AND SPORES

RAGWEED POLLEN

SPORES OF SCOURING RUSH

Pollen grains have different shapes in different kinds of plants. Spores resist changes in heat and cold.

lilacs and willow, plum, cherry and peach trees. The mildew covers these plants with a mycelium through which it draws nourishment from the plant's cells. This destroys these cells, and therefore, kills the plant.

Observe mildew plants in the same way that you observed molds.

When you were feeding protozoa, you **What is yeast budding?** made a mixture of yeast and water. Although you were primarily interested in the protozoa, you may have noticed that the yeast cells had many curious shapes. Let us again observe yeast. As before, mix a tiny speck of yeast in a drop of water. Place a cover glass on the mixture. Manipulate the mirror of your microscope so as to cut down the light, and focus carefully on the yeast.

Yeast is a plant. The round, or nearly-round, cells that you see are each a separate yeast plant. Two things that will probably catch your attention immediately are that some yeast cells seem to have lumps sticking out of them, and that yeast cells are seen in chains. These two facts are closely related.

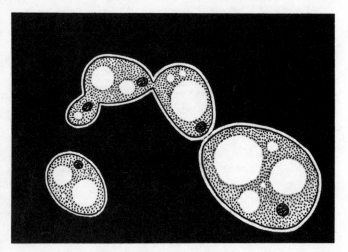

Yeast cells reproduce by a division called "budding."

Like other cells, yeast plants reproduce by cell division. But instead of dividing in two in the middle, a yeast cell grows a bud. This bud is the lump that you can see attached to some cells. Just as in other kinds of cell division, the nucleus splits in two. One part of the nucleus moves into the bud, and the other part remains in the parent cell. The bud is small at first, but soon grows to be the same size as the cell from which it budded. As you will remember, this is quite different from the type of cell division you have observed. There, the cell pinched in two, forming two cells each half the size of the cell that divided. Each of the two new cells then grew to the size of the cell from which they came.

Another way in which the budding of

How else does yeast budding differ from cell division?

yeast cells differs from most cell division is in the fact that the new cell which grows from the bud does not necessarily separate from the parent cell. Although the parent cell and the budded cell live as separate plants, they may remain attached to each other. As both these cells bud in turn, and the buds grow to full size, a chain of four cells is formed. Even longer chains of yeast cells may be formed. However, the connection between the cells is not very strong, and, eventually, the chain breaks.

If you search about among the yeast cells on your slide, you may find cells that have more than one bud. When this kind of budding takes place, Y-shaped chains may be formed.

There are thousands of different kinds

How are yeasts useful to man?

of yeasts. Certain kinds are very useful to man. These are the ones used in the process of *fermentation*. Most yeasts live and grow on sugar. As they obtain their nourishment from sugar, they change it into alcohol and carbon dioxide gas. This is the process called *fermentation*. Alcohol is a very useful chemical.

When yeast is mixed with baking dough, the yeast plants grow on the sugar in the dough. That is, the yeast ferments the sugar in the dough to form alcohol and carbon dioxide. This gas forms bubbles in the dough, and the dough swells. When this happens we say that the dough "rises." Dough that rises becomes light and fluffy. When the bread is baked, the heat drives off both the carbon dioxide and the alcohol. All the holes and indentations in a slice of bread are the remains of bubbles of carbon dioxide.

Dissolve a teaspoonful of sugar in half a tumbler of water. Make up a fresh mixture of yeast and water. Place a drop of the mixture on a cover glass and add a drop of sugar-water. Make a hanging-drop preparation of the cover glass and its mixture. Leave the hanging-drop slide in a warm place. An hour later, place the slide under your microscope. Do you see the many bubbles of carbon dioxide formed by the yeast's fermenting action on the sugar?

How can you see fermentation?

Insects

Obtain a small wide-mouth bottle with a lid. Cover the inside bottom with blotting paper, paper towels or absorbent cotton. Then wet the material with household ammonia. (Do not hold your face close to the bottle when you are pouring ammonia, for it will cause your eyes and nose to smart painfully.) Cap the wide-mouth bottle. Now you have an insect collector's bottle. If you place an insect in it, the ammonia will quickly kill the specimen without damaging it as swatting might do.

Where can you keep insects?

Catch a fly in your hand. When you see a fly resting on some object, slowly move your cupped hand close to the insect. Then, with a sudden quick movement, grab the fly. You will probably have to try this more than once. Hold the fly gently in your hand, and then pop it into the collecting bottle. After the fly is dead, use your tweezers to remove it from the bottle. Place it on a glass slide and manipulate it with your probe so that you can obtain a good view of one of its eyes beneath the low-power objective of your microscope.

Do you see that the whole surface of the eye is composed of tiny hexagonal (six-sided) spaces? These spaces are called *facets*. Each one gives the fly a separate impression of light and color. In other words, each facet acts as though it were a separate eye. An eye made up of facets is called a compound eye. Many insects have such eyes.

What does a fly's eye look like?

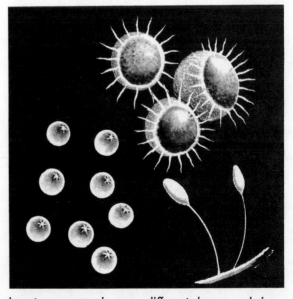

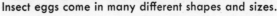

Insect eggs come in many different shapes and sizes.

39

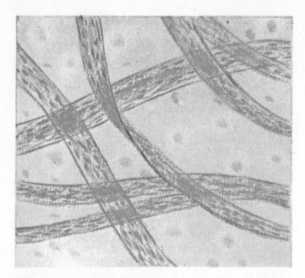
Orlon acrylic fiber, as seen under a microscope.

A filament of rayon yarn as seen under a microscope.

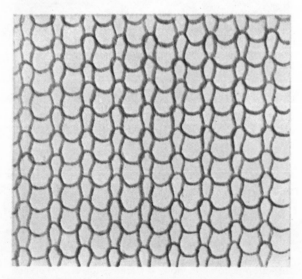
Nylon stocking weave as seen under microscope.

Note how the fly's eye bulges outward on all sides of the head. In fact the eyes make up the largest part of the head. Because the eyes bulge out so far, they enable the fly to see in all directions at once. This is why it is so hard to catch a fly, for it can see as well behind as in front of itself.

Look at the fly's foot. Note the hairy pads between two curving claws. The pads secrete a sticky substance that enable the fly to cling to smooth surfaces. This is why a fly can walk upside down on the ceiling. Look at the wings of a fly. The "veins" in the wing are really dried-up air tubes that connect with the fly's breathing organs.

How can a fly walk upside down?

There are more kinds of insects than any other kind of animal. As insects have an almost infinite variety of forms and oddly-shaped organs, a collection of several different kinds will provide you with enough material for many hours of interesting microscopic examination.

Fabrics

You may already know that cotton thread is made from the cotton plant. The fruit of the cotton plant is a white fluffy material much like absorbent cotton. This is cleaned and spun into thread. But just what goes on in the spinning process? You can find this out by examining a piece

How is cotton thread made?

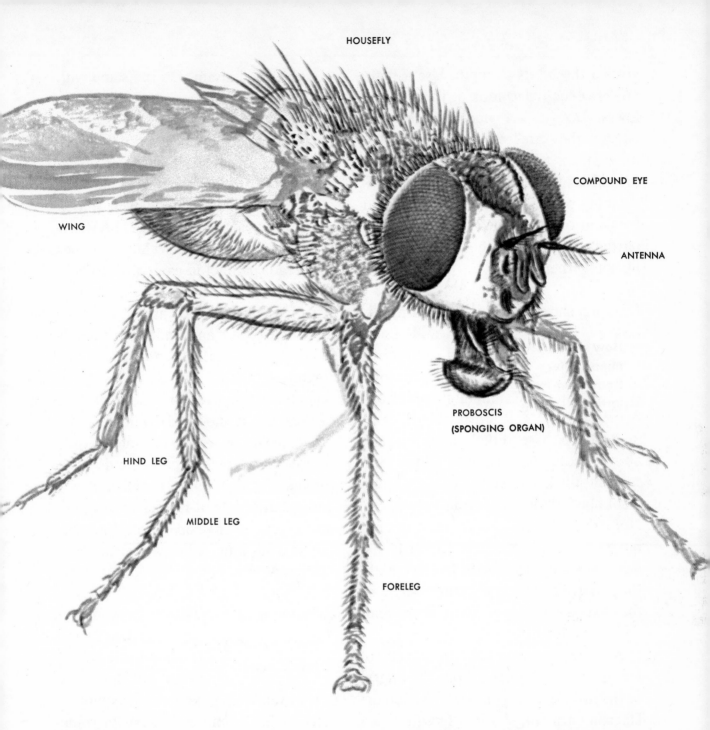

COMPOUND EYE

ANTENNA

WING

PROBOSCIS
(SPONGING ORGAN)

HIND LEG

MIDDLE LEG

FORELEG

of cotton thread under your microscope.

Make another probe by sticking the eye-end of a needle into the eraser from a pencil. Cut a half-inch length of cotton thread, wet it, and place it on a slide beneath the low-power objective of your microscope. Note that the whole length of the thread has a spiral twist.

Using both your probes, pick the thread apart. First undo the spiral, then pick the strands apart into the smaller fibers of which they are made. When you have taken the whole piece of thread apart, you can easily reconstruct what went on in the spinning process. The fibers that make up the cotton as it comes from the plant were pulled out into strands which were then twisted into a thread.

Since it is so easy to pick apart a piece of cotton, you may wonder what gives a thread its strength. Use a high-power objective to look at the smallest fibers. Do you see how crooked and twisted they are? When a number of these fibers are brought in close contact with one another, as in the cotton-spinning process, the crooked parts and bends of one fiber catch in the crooked parts of another and hold the separate fiber together.

Obtain a short length of wool yarn, silk thread and linen thread. Examine **How do natural fibers differ from man-made (artificial) ones?** each under the low- and high-power objectives of your microscope. Use direct lighting from above. Note that the wool fibers are straight, thick and scaly. Compare these wool fibers with a hair from your head. Note that the silk fibers are straight, but have rough surfaces. Linen fibers have very jagged surfaces. Do you think that there is any connection between the jagged surface of linen fibers and the strength of linen thread?

All the fibers you have examined so far are natural fibers. From the edges of the inside of a rayon, nylon, Orlon or Dacron garment, obtain a few threads. These are artificial or man-made fibers. Examine them under your microscope. Note how smooth they are when compared to natural fibers.

You can keep an interesting record of what you have learned by placing half-inch lengths of the four kinds of natural fibers on a glass slide, carefully covering them with a thin coating of Canada balsam and placing a cover glass on the balsam. Do the same with the four kinds of man-made fibers.

Look at a muslin sheet or pillowcase **How is muslin woven?** with the low-power objective. Note how evenly the threads are woven into a square pattern. The weaving is done by stretching a large number of threads parallel to each other. These threads make the *warp*. An equal number of parallel threads are woven over and under, over and under the threads of the warp. The second group of threads is called the *woof,* or *weft.* Sometimes the over-and-under pattern of weaving is modified by having the woof go over two, three or more threads of the warp, before going under one thread. Try to obtain examples of rep and gabardine twill fabrics to examine under your microscope. Note how different from muslin the weave of these fabrics is.

Examine a jersey, T-shirt, or woman's **How is knitted fabric made?** stocking. The fabric from which these items are made is not woven, but is knitted. Examine a piece of felt from a man's hat or some other source. Can you see a weaving pattern here? There is none, for felt is not a woven cloth. It is made from a large number of short fur fibers that are mixed with water. The water is drained off, and the resulting mat is pressed flat.

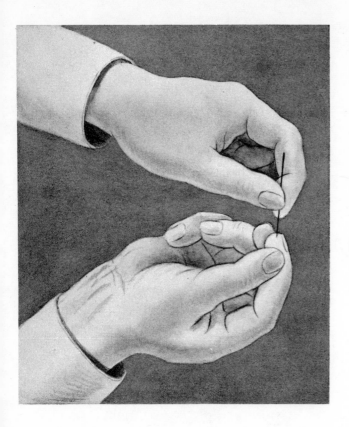

You can obtain a blood sample from the index finger of your hand with a sterilized needle.

Below are three steps in making a blood smear on a slide as indicated on page 44.

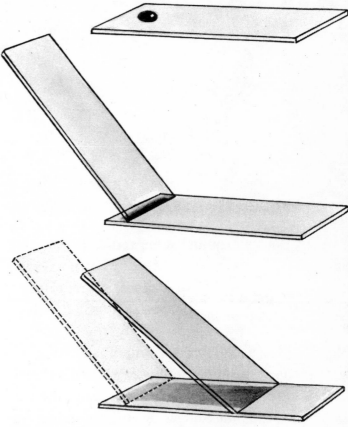

Blood

What does blood do? One of the most interesting things you can examine under a microscope is your own blood. Blood is a most remarkable fluid. It has been called "the river of life," and this is an excellent description, for blood supplies the cells of the body with the materials they need for nourishment and repair, and it removes wastes from the cells. Also, the blood contains cells that fight disease and substances that repair cut or bruised parts of the body.

What is blood made of? Blood is made up of both liquid and solid parts. The liquid is called *plasma*. The solid parts are *red corpuscles, white corpuscles,* and *platelets.* The word *corpuscle* is the Latin word for "little body." Corpuscles are cells. More than nine-tenths of the blood consists of red corpuscles. These cells are so small that a large drop of blood contains more than 250 million of them. They are disc-shaped and concave on each side, and contain a substance called *hemoglobin.* When hemoglobin combines with oxygen, it turns bright red. This is why fresh blood outside the body is always red.

43

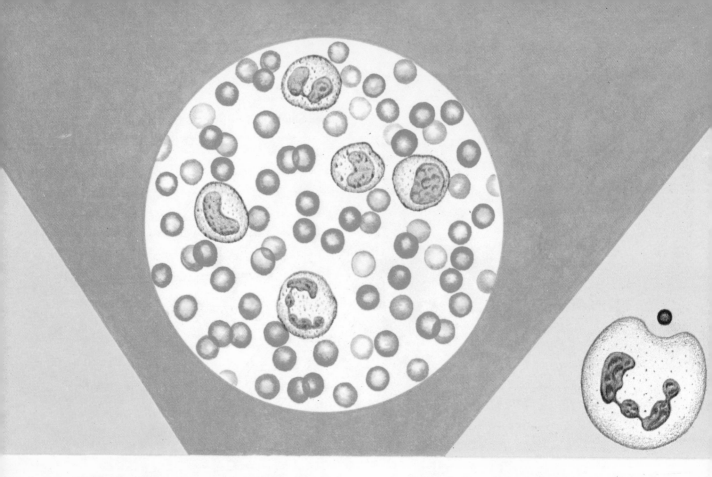

Let us examine some red cells. Set out

How can you get a sample of your blood? two clean glass slides, some absorbent cotton, a bottle of hydrogen peroxide (usually called simply "peroxide"), a candle, a pair of tweezers, and a sharp needle. Light the candle. Scrub the tip of the index finger of your left hand (if you are right-handed) with a swab of peroxide-soaked cotton. Be thorough about this, in order to kill all bacteria on your fingertip. Hold this finger firmly between the thumb and middle finger of the same hand. Grasp the needle with the tweezers. Now, sterilize the point of the needle by holding it in the candle flame for 20 seconds. When the needle has cooled, grasp it near, but not at, the point. Quickly jab the needle into the index finger of your left hand — the one you have cleaned. This will hurt no more than a mosquito

bite. Squeeze your finger in order to form a large drop of blood above the puncture. Before you go about taking a drop of your own blood, however, be sure to get permission from your parent or guardian. Also, you must be sure to have an adult supervise your whole experiment.

With your right hand, pick up one of

How do you make a blood smear? the clean slides and touch it, near one end, to the drop of blood. Place this slide on a table, with the drop of blood uppermost. Hold this slide firmly between the thumb and middle finger of your left hand. Pick up the other slide in your right hand. Hold it nearly vertical and touch its bottom edge to the drop of blood on the first slide. Rapidly and smoothly move the nearly-vertical slide along the surface of the other slide,

44

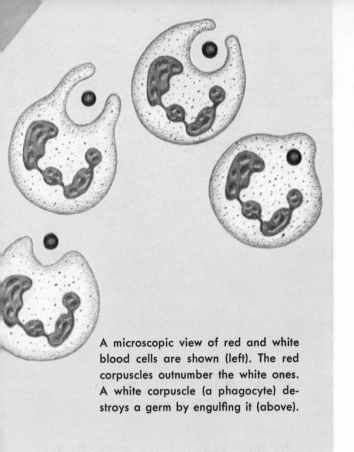

A microscopic view of red and white blood cells are shown (left). The red corpuscles outnumber the white ones. A white corpuscle (a phagocyte) destroys a germ by engulfing it (above).

cells standing on edge and resembling dumbbells. There may be several red cells stacked one on top of another like a pile of coins.

Here and there among the red cells, you will see a much larger, colorless cell. These are white corpuscles. There is only one white corpuscle for approximately every 800 red corpuscles. Most of these cells have a generally round shape, but they may be in almost any shape, looking very much like an amoeba. In fact, they are able to move through the body's tissues in much the same manner as an amoeba moves. White cells are the body's disease fighters, and disease is caused by an overabundance of harmful bacteria within

pulling the blood in an even smear along behind the moving slide. Study the illustration to understand clearly how to do this. You must do all this quickly, so that the drop of blood on the slide does not clot before you spread it out into a smear.

When you have finished making the blood smear, swab off your left index finger with peroxide-soaked cotton.

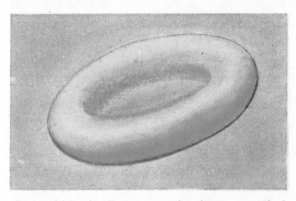

One red blood cell, or corpuscle, shown magnified.

Examine the blood smear under the low-power objective.

What do blood cells look like? The red cells will look barely pink. Move the slide back and forth in order to get an idea of how many thousands of red cells are in the small drop of blood you put on the slide.

Now, use the high-power objective. You can easily see that red cells are circular with a concave depression in the middle of each side. You may see some

the body. It is the task of white corpuscles to destroy bacteria. To destroy a bacterium, a white cell engulfs it, just as an amoeba engulfs a bit of food. Inside the white cell, the bacterium is digested.

A special kind of stain is needed to properly stain a white cell, but you can do a fairly good job by using "permanent" blue fountain pen ink. When you have fixed and stained your blood smear, you will see that white corpuscles have very irregularly-shaped nuclei. The nucleus may be round, somewhat horse-shoe-shaped, or made up of several small bits held together by threads of nuclear material. It is because of the shape of the nucleus, that a white cell is called a *polymorphonuclear leucocyte*. *Poly* means "many" in Greek; *morphos* means "form"; *leuco* means "white"; and *cytos* means "cell." Thus, the big word means "white cell with many-formed nucleus."

How can you see blood in circulation? Get a piece of thin wood about three inches long and two inches wide. A piece of plywood will do, or a shingle. Near one end, drill a hole about a half-inch in diameter. Make a pad of wet cloth or

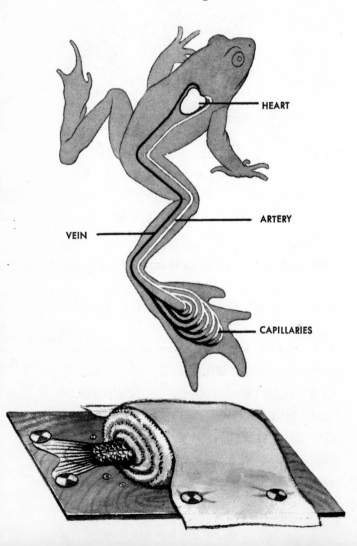

HEART

ARTERY

VEIN

CAPILLARIES

absorbent cotton about five by ten inches. Gently wrap a live goldfish in this pad, so that only its tail sticks out. Put the fish on the board in such a position that the tail-fin is directly over the hole. Place a handkerchief over the upper part of the fish and fix the handkerchief to the board with thumbtacks. Place two other thumbtacks at the edges of the hole so that the edges of the tacks press on the two outer points of the fish's tail. Be careful not to stick the tacks through the tail.

Place the board on the stage of your microscope, with the tail directly under the objective. Focus with low power. As you examine the tail, wet it from time to time with a little water from your fingers.

You will see large blood vessels that run parallel to the rays of the tail. Note how these large vessels divide into smaller branches, and these branches into tiny ones, called *capillaries*. If you follow the flow of blood cells from the large blood vessels to the capillaries, you will see that from the capillaries, the blood flows into larger branches that join still larger blood vessels, as the blood flows back to the fish's heart.

Do not keep the fish out of water for more than ten minutes. If, when you return the fish to water, it seems sluggish and unable to swim well, pick it up by the tail and dip it in and out of the water a few times. This should help the fish to begin breathing properly again.

The flow of blood may be viewed in a frog's foot as it travels from the heart, through the arteries and capillaries and back to the heart through the veins. The blood flow may also be viewed in a fish's tail.

Suppose you are interested in learning

How can you observe the insides of living things?
about the heart of a frog, the stem of a flower, or the egg of an insect. After you have examined these objects with the low- and high-power objectives of your microscope, you can still learn much more about them by studying their insides. What is the best way to do this?

Obtain a bolt that is at least one-quarter inch in diameter, and a nut to fit the bolt. Screw the bolt about one-quarter way into the nut. Prop the bolt in a vertical position, so that the opening in the bolt is uppermost. Place the object you wish to study inside this opening. Melt some paraffin — the material used to seal jam and jelly jars — in a spoon, using a candle flame for a source of heat. Pour the melted paraffin into the hole in the bolt.

When the paraffin has cooled and hardened, slowly screw the bolt farther into the nut, thereby pushing out some paraffin. When about 1/64 of an inch (or less) of paraffin has been pushed out, move a razor blade down along the face of the bolt, so as to cut off a thin

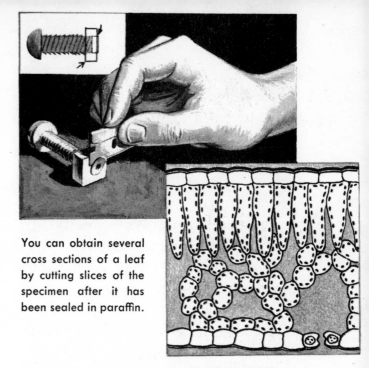

You can obtain several cross sections of a leaf by cutting slices of the specimen after it has been sealed in paraffin.

slice of paraffin. If this slice contains a portion of your specimen, place the slice on a slide and examine it under the microscope. If not, then push out another 1/64 of an inch of paraffin. Continue this until one of the slices contains a piece of the specimen. Then, go on making more slices until you have passed from one end to the other of the specimen. Each slice shows you a cross section, revealing what is inside the object under study.

If your specimen is too large to be put into the hole in a bolt, use some other small container, such as a match box.

The Electron Microscope

Both the simple and compound micro-

What are the limitations of optical microscopes?
scopes are called *optical* microscopes. They both use light to present an enlarged image to the eye. But no matter how powerful optical micro-
scopes are made, there is a limit to the smallness of the object that they can magnify. We learned that light must be reflected from an object in order for it to be seen. Objects also can be seen when they stop the passage of light, as when they make a shadow; and also

when they partially stop the passages of light, as when light passes up from a microscope's mirror through the body of a protozoan. Light rays have a certain definite size, and they cannot be reflected from or stopped by objects that are smaller than the rays themselves. To try to see objects that are smaller than the light rays is like trying to catch minnows with a mackerel net.

A scientist operates a powerful electron microscope.

If we could have some kind of ray, or beam, that could be reflected from objects too small to reflect light, we could see these objects. There are tiny particles, called *electrons*, that are sufficiently small for our purpose. Scientists have worked out a way to use a beam of electrons in a microscope. This microscope is called an *electron microscope*.

What is an electron microscope?

By heating a certain kind of wire, a large number of electrons may be obtained. Electrons are electrically charged particles. By using magnets in exactly the same way an optical microscope uses lenses, the electrons obtained from the wire can be formed into a beam, to be directed and magnified.

Since eyesight requires light, we cannot look into an electron microscope as we do an optical one. But the beam of electrons can form an image on photographic film. When the film is developed, we see what was beneath the electron microscope's objective.

With this instrument, we can get magnifications of more than 200 thousand times, but because an electron microscope costs several thousand dollars, it is usually found only in university and industrial research laboratories.

One of the great triumphs of the electron microscope has been to reveal viruses, the smallest living things. Viruses cause many diseases, among which are measles, mumps, chickenpox, smallpox, rabies and polio. The electron microscope may help us to conquer disease by enabling us to work with viruses.

How does this microscope help man?

You have learned something about the world of very small things that exist all around us. You have learned about a wonderful instrument, the microscope, that has enabled man to enter this tiny world. You have learned how to use a microscope and how to obtain and prepare very small specimens so that you can observe them with this important instrument.

But if what you have learned has aroused an interest in the "unseen world," then ahead of you are endless, invaluable hours of fun and learning.

THE HOW AND WHY WONDER BOOK OF
CHEMISTRY

Written by MARTIN L. KEEN
Illustrated by WALTER FERGUSON
Cover Illustration by DONALD CROWLEY
Editorial Production: DONALD D. WOLF

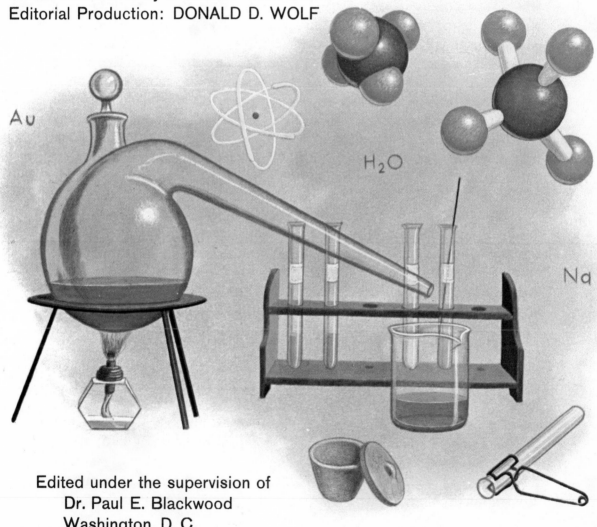

Au

H₂O

Na

Edited under the supervision of
    Dr. Paul E. Blackwood
    Washington, D. C.

Text and illustrations approved by
    Oakes A. White, Brooklyn Children's Museum, Brooklyn, New York

GROSSET & DUNLAP • **Publishers** • **NEW YORK**

Introduction

What are things made of? This is the big question which *The How and Why Wonder Book of Chemistry* deals with. There are so many kinds of materials in our world that the question is not easily answered. But for centuries people have tried to find the answer. The search has been long and fascinating from the time of the alchemists down to the modern atomic scientist.

Once it was believed that all things were made of some combination of earth, air, fire and water. Little by little new discoveries were made. Now we know that instead of just four "building blocks," there are at least 103 different ones! This *How and Why Wonder Book* tells how scientists have made some of the discoveries along the historic path of chemistry. And it records the answers to many questions that have always puzzled people.

More than that, the reader gets a feeling of the unanswered puzzles of nature which challenge scientists to continue their explorations. How is it, for example, that carbon, a common element, appears in so many forms? Sometimes it is soot from the chimney; again it is graphite, the "lead" in an ordinary pencil; or perhaps, most surprising of all, it is sometimes the brilliant and lovely diamond! Equally astonishing is that a green gas and a silvery metal solid may combine to make a white solid — ordinary table salt!

Of special interest to many readers will be several chemical experiments in the book, which may be done at home or in school. The experiments will enable young scientists to rediscover some of the facts about matter while working with materials the way chemists do. Whether chemistry deals with metals or non-metals, with acids, bases and salts, with foods, drugs, plastics, or with living or non-living things, it always goes back to one basic thing: *matter*. Since this book deals with many of these subjects, it is really an introductory reference work for all young students interested in chemistry. It is an essential title in the growing list of *How and Why Wonder Books*.

Paul E. Blackwood

Dr. Blackwood is a professional employee in the U. S. Office of Education. This book was edited by him in his private capacity and no official support or endorsement by the Office of Education is intended or should be inferred.

Library of Congress Catalog Card Number: 61-12932

Contents

Early man probably got his knowledge of fire from the world of nature around him. From his observations of erupting volcanoes, and fires caused by lightning and sunlight, man soon discovered that fire could be put to useful purposes. Thus, he might be considered the first chemist, and it is a fascinating journey from that day to the role of present-day chemistry.

What Is Chemistry?

It is impossible to look around your home without seeing some of the things chemistry had a part in making. It was chemists who learned how to make the plaster that covers the inside walls. Perhaps the walls are painted. Chemists directed the making of oils and color in the paint.

Probably some of your clothes, the rugs, the curtains or the covering of your chair or sofa are woven of rayon, nylon or some other one of the man-made fibers that chemists have developed.

In the kitchen are foods that were bought in fresh condition because chemists made materials to preserve the foods

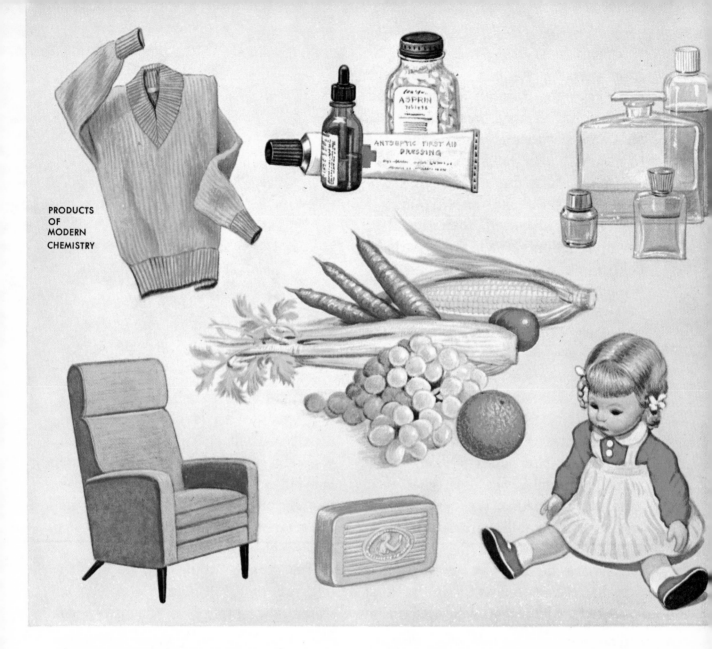

PRODUCTS OF MODERN CHEMISTRY

from rotting. Chemists also made sprays that the food growers used to kill worms and other insects that might have eaten into the fruits and vegetables. Perhaps at this very moment some food is being cooked in your home. Cooking is a kind of chemistry.

In your bathroom are soaps and medicines that would have been impossible to produce if their makers did not have a knowledge of chemistry.

You probably have had toys made of plastic materials. Plastics would not even exist but for the science of chemistry.

If it were not for chemistry, the paper on which this book is printed would be a dirty, speckled brown, so that you could hardly read the words on it. And the ink in which these words are printed was made by chemists.

If you think about all these things in which chemistry had a part in making, you will see that none of them is found as such in nature. None can be grown on plants or trees, nor obtained from parts of animals, nor dug from the earth. Where, then, did they come from? Chemists took materials that *are* grown on plants and trees, obtained from parts of animals, dug from the earth or taken from air or water; and the chemists changed these natural materials into other materials — the ones from which the things in your home are made. It is this *changing of one kind of material into another* that is the chief business of chemistry. For example, nylon is made from parts of coal, air and water, and some paints are made from parts of soybeans.

There is one other main task of chemistry: to carefully describe the many materials and their parts. A chemist who discovers or makes a certain material must describe that material carefully so that other chemists can recognize or make the new material themselves. How does a chemist describe materials? He tells what their colors are, whether they are light or heavy, shiny or dull, hard or soft. He is careful to tell whether the material is a solid, a liquid or a gas. He tells whether the material will sink or float in water, whether it will dissolve in water, in alcohol or in other liquids, how it will act when heated and many other things. These things are called the *properties* of the material.

Let us see how this knowledge might be of use. Suppose you had two glass jars, one filled with salt and the other with clean white sand. Suppose you did not know which jar was filled with salt and which with sand. You would not want to put sand on your food, so you would have to find some way of telling what was in each jar.

As you looked at each jar you would see that its contents appear just about like that of the other jar. So, just look-

ing would be of no help. Suppose, then, you were to ask a chemist which is heavier — salt or sand. He would tell you that sand is heavier, but so little heavier that it wouldn't do much good to take one jar in one hand and the other jar in the other hand, and try to feel which is heavier.

The chemist would also be able to tell you that salt easily dissolves in water, while sand does not dissolve at all. Now, knowing this, all you have to do is to take a pinch of material from one of your jars, drop it into a glass of water, and stir. If the material dissolves, it is salt; if not, it is sand.

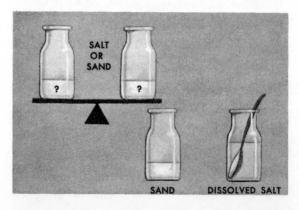

Salt will dissolve in water; sand will not dissolve.

Perfume was known in ancient Egypt. The picture, after a tomb painting, shows women preparing perfume.

The ancient Egyptians were casting bronze in 1500 B.C. The illustration, after a painting on the wall of an Egyptian tomb, shows workmen lifting a crucible to fill containers with the metal. In the background is a furnace, and on the floor, foot-operated bellows.

ALCHEMIST'S EQUIPMENT

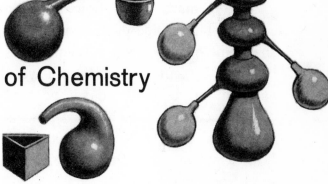

The Ancestors of Chemistry

How did chemistry begin?

Men were making use of chemistry long before they knew anything about the science of chemistry. For example, the ancient Egyptians, more than 3,000 years ago, had learned skill in working iron. This metal is found in the earth combined with other materials to make a reddish brown rock-like material. In this form, it is called iron ore. For the Egyptians to separate the metal from the rest of the iron ore required a real use of chemistry. The Egyptians and several other ancient peoples who lived on the shores of the Mediterranean Sea mined silver, gold, lead, tin and copper. They knew how to combine copper and tin to form bronze, a metal that is quite hard, but from which it is easy to make things.

Ancient peoples made spears, swords, helmets, bells, horns, chariots, chairs, pots, pans and a host of other things from bronze. To combine copper and tin in just the right amounts for making bronze was a skill that also required a use of chemistry.

The ancient Egyptians could make glass, tile, turpentine, soap and dyes. To make any of these things requires the use of chemistry. So good were the Egyptians at making them that some of their colored glass and tile have been dug up from the earth where they were buried for thousands of years — and the colors are as bright as when

7

the glass and tile decorated the palaces of Egyptian pharaohs. Egyptian pictures in colored tile show ships with bright-colored stripes dyed in their sails, and nobles, both men and women, wearing beautifully colored clothes. All these facts are still more evidence that the Egyptians knew how to do things that required the use of chemistry.

The Romans knew how to make cement. They made such good cement that some of their roads and aqueducts, built of cement two thousand years ago, can still be used today. The hardening of cement is a chemical process. This shows that the Romans, too, knew how to make materials that required the use of chemistry.

Empedocles: all things are made of four elements

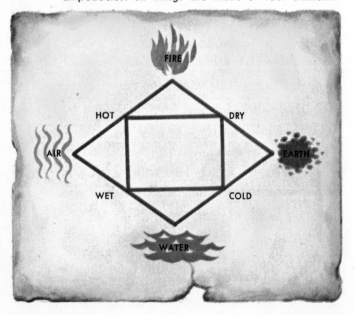

An ancient Greek wise man named Empedocles taught that all materials are made of four things called *elements:* earth, air, water and fire. For two thousand years after Empedocles, certain men tried to make different kinds of materials by combining these four elements in different ways. Fortunately, for the future of chemistry, these men thought of earth as including anything solid, such as ore, metal, salt, glass or wood. Also, they counted any kind of gas as air and any liquid as water.

8

Jugs of colored water, symbolic colors originated by the alchemists, are still used today in modern pharmacies and drugstores as a professional sign.

What these men were most interested in doing was to

How did chemistry get its name?

change cheap metals, such as tin, iron and lead, into gold. Where did they get the idea that less valuable metals could be turned into gold? The idea came from another ancient Greek, Aristotle, who had written that all things had the possibility of becoming perfect. Gold was considered to be the only perfect metal, and many people reasoned that less perfect metals could be changed into gold — if one could only learn how. And if one *could* learn how, men of olden times thought, what a wonderful way to become rich! The man who could learn the secret of changing a metal like lead into gold would soon be richer than anyone else. It was not hard to get hundreds of pounds of lead, but very few men owned even an ounce of gold.

The work of trying to change less valuable metals into gold was called *alchemy*, and the men who did this work were *alchemists*. It was from these words that we got our modern words *chemistry* and *chemist*. Because of the work they were doing, alchemists were given the nickname of "gold cooks." In the courts of many kings and nobles, the gold cooks held an honored place. One emperor built, near his palace, six small stone houses with large furnaces for the use of the royal alchemists. King Henry VI of England told his noblemen and scholars that alchemy was a valuable study that they should all learn.

Besides gold, there were two other things that alchemists tried to make in their laboratories. One was a liquid that would dissolve anything. They never stopped to think that such a liquid would also dissolve any bottle or other container in which they tried to keep it. The other thing they sought was a drink that would make old people young, and would cause all who drank it to live forever.

For hundreds of years alchemists worked in vain, never discovering any of the things they sought. They worked in smoke-blackened laboratories filled with the strange fumes and odors given off by the liquids they boiled and the powders they burned. The stone walls were covered with mysterious signs that were supposed to have magic powers. The red light of the fires in the alche-

mists' furnaces cast weird shadows and made eerie gleams dance on the odd-shaped glassware in which the gold cooks heated and stored their brews.

Alchemists found that a number of materials were especially useful in their work. Also, they discovered some new materials. They wanted to keep their knowledge of these materials secret from all except other alchemists. To do this, alchemists devised a number of signs, or *symbols,* that stood for the names of the metals and other substances with which they worked.

What were alchemical symbols?

Following are the signs that alchemists painted on the walls of their laboratories. Alchemists liked to believe that their symbols made alchemy seem mysteriously important to those who were not alchemists. In addition to the alchemical symbols are the materials the symbols stand for:

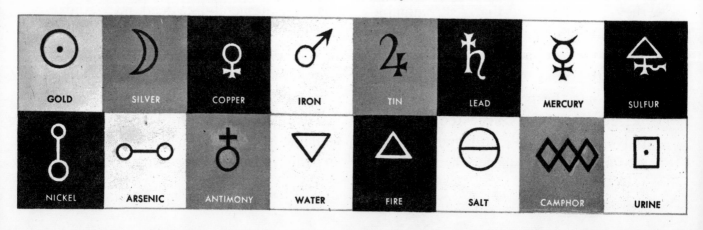

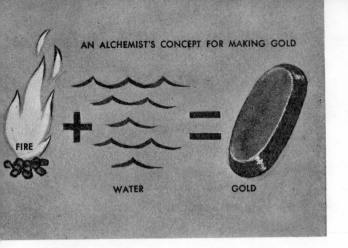

AN ALCHEMIST'S CONCEPT FOR MAKING GOLD

FIRE + WATER = GOLD

Some alchemists were dishonest. They cleverly hid small lumps of gold in their furnaces.

What happened to alchemy?

Then, in the presence of those from whom they got money, the alchemists "discovered" the gold in the ashes of one of their experiments. And then, they claimed that if they were given more money for more experiments, surely a way would be found to get really large lumps of gold out of the ashes.

Other alchemists were honest. In the hundreds of years of their fruitless experimenting, they gathered a long list of useful facts about their work. They described the ways in which many materials acted when mixed together or heated or shaken. They learned which liquids would dissolve metals and other materials, and which liquids would dissolve in others. They recorded the weights and colors and many other facts.

It is only about two hundred years since the last alchemist gave up his hopeless search. But the information gathered by him and the alchemists who lived earlier made up a store of knowledge, some of which became the basis for the true science of chemistry.

The Language of Chemistry

Every science has words that describe things and ideas with which the science deals. The words chemists use when they talk about their work are called "chemical terms," and they are important to know if we are to understand the science of chemistry.

Anything that has weight is matter.

nose, ice cream, a rock, water, milk, air, the sun, moon and stars are all examples of matter.

Are there any things that are not matter? Yes. Radio waves and television waves and heat are among the things that have no weight, and therefore are not matter. Also, ideas and feelings are things, but they are not matter. Patriotism, love, sadness, memories and daydreams have no weight and are not matter.

MATTER

The first word is *matter*. When a chemist talks about matter, he means anything that has weight. Anything you can see or touch is matter. This book, your

What is matter?

GAS

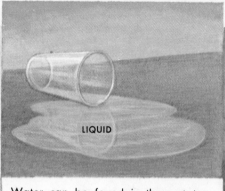
LIQUID

SOLID

Water can be found in three states.

The objects in the world about us seem to be made up of an endless number of different kinds of matter.

What are the three states of matter?

Things are made of wood, paper, metal, rubber, cloth, plastic and a host of other materials. There is rough and smooth matter, hard and soft matter — and all matter appears in a great variety of colors and shapes. There are millions of different kinds of matter. Yet, a chemist separates all matter into three divisions: matter that is *solid*, matter that is *liquid* and matter that is *gas*. Each one of these large divisions of matter is called a *state of matter*. A rock and a baseball are examples of matter in the solid state. Water, milk and gasoline represent matter in the liquid state. Air is matter in the state of a gas.

If you place an ice cube in a glass half full of water, you can see all three states of matter at one time. The ice is solid, the water is liquid and the air above the water is gas.

Place two or three ice cubes into an empty teakettle.

How can you change one state of matter into another state?

Put the kettle on a burner of a gas range. Keep the flame of the burner low and leave the lid off the kettle. What happens inside the kettle? The ice melts; that is, it changes to water. Here, you see a solid changing to a liquid.

Put the lid on the kettle and turn the burner up higher. When the water in the kettle boils, look at the spout from the side. Between the spout and the steam, you will see a clear space. In this space is *water vapor;* that is, water in the form of a gas. (Do not try to touch the water vapor! It is very hot, and will give you a bad burn.)

The steam, which begins to appear just in front of the water vapor, is made up of tiny droplets of water. Upon leaving the spout, the water vapor came in contact with the cooler air, and the gas (water vapor) changed to a liquid (water). If you want to prove that cooling water vapor changes to water, wrap a towel around the handle of a tablespoon and hold the bowl of the spoon in the water vapor. (Be careful!) Drops of water will collect on the spoon.

If you should put the water that collects on the spoon into the freezing compartment of a refrigerator, the water would turn to ice. Thus, you would have an example of matter in the liquid state turning to matter in the solid state.

Most kinds of matter can exist in each

of the three states. Iron can be melted and, thereby, changed from the solid to the liquid state. The iron becomes liquid when it is heated to 2,800 degrees Fahrenheit. (The usual temperature inside a house is about 70 degrees Fahrenheit.) If liquid iron is heated further, until its temperature reaches 5,400 degrees Fahrenheit, the iron boils and becomes a gas.

You have probably noticed the bubbles in soda. These bubbles are made of *carbon dioxide,* a harmless gas. If you were to put some of this gas into the proper kind of container, and then lower the temperature to 69 degrees below zero Fahrenheit, the carbon dioxide gas would turn to liquid carbon dioxide. If you cooled the liquid carbon dioxide further, until its temperature dropped to 110 degrees below zero Fahrenheit, the liquid would become solid. Perhaps you have seen solid carbon dioxide. It is called "dry ice," and is used by street vendors of ice cream to keep their wares cold.

You have probably guessed that by changing the temperature of matter, you can change it from one state to another. This is true. Heating and cooling matter are the main ways chemists use to change it from one state to another.

Tanning animal hides makes them into leather by causing a chemical change that prevents rotting. After soaking hides in salt water to remove dirt and blood, ancient tanners rubbed the hides with lime to remove the hair. The limed hides were washed and hung on sticks in vats of tanning solution made by soaking bark, leaves, wood or nuts in water. The leather was rubbed with oil to make it soft. This process has been replaced by new methods (right).

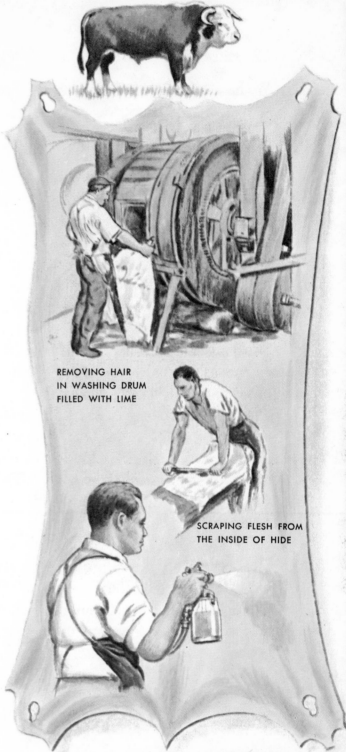

REMOVING HAIR IN WASHING DRUM FILLED WITH LIME

SCRAPING FLESH FROM THE INSIDE OF HIDE

SPRAYING WITH BETA NAPHTOL TO DESTROY HIDE-ATTACKING BACTERIA

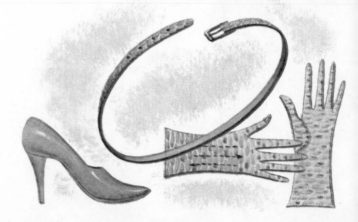

CHEMICAL ELEMENTS

What is a chemical element? We have learned that the ancient Greek, Empedocles, said the elements of which all things are made are earth, air, water and fire. Now an element of anything is a part so simple that it cannot be divided into any simpler parts. When alchemists worked with various solid materials that they believed to be forms of the element *earth*, they soon learned that many of these solid materials could be separated into simpler materials. This proved that *earth* was not really an element. On the other hand, alchemists found that certain materials — almost all of them metals — could not be separated into simpler parts. These indivisible materials were true *chemical elements*. The elements the alchemists knew were gold, silver, copper, iron, lead, tin, mercury, antimony, sulfur, arsenic, phosphorus and carbon. You have probably recognized that many of these are names of metals known to the ancient Egyptians, who also knew of sulfur and carbon.

Mercury was probably discovered about the year A.D. 300 by a Greek named Theophrastus, while the elements arsenic and antimony were discovered in the Middle Ages.

In the eighteenth century, when chemistry was becoming a science, chemists began to discover new chemical elements. The discovery of elements went on until chemists had found 92 elements in materials gotten from the earth and the air. Then, recently, chemists learned how to make new chemical elements, and have made eleven more for a total of 103 elements. On page 15 of this book you will find a list of all the chemical elements discovered up to the time these words were written.

It is an important fact that chemical elements are the simplest kinds of matter with which a chemist works.

CHEMICAL SYMBOLS

What are chemical symbols? Following the name of each element in the list on page 15, you will see one or two letters. For instance, following *calcium* are the letters *Ca*. These letters are an abbreviation of the name of the element. Chemists find that using these abbreviations is easier

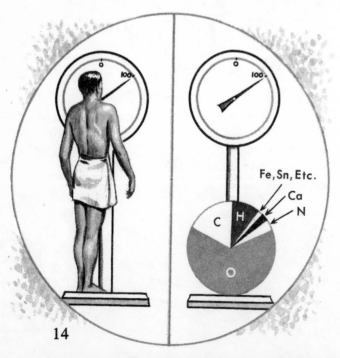

If you weigh 100 pounds, your body is made up of roughly 65 pounds of oxygen, 18 pounds of carbon, 10 pounds of hydrogen, 3 pounds of nitrogen, 2 pounds of calcium, 1 pound of phosphorus. The remaining pound consists of iron, zinc, potassium, sodium, chlorine, fluorine, bromine, iodine, magnesium, manganese, copper, chromium, molybdenum, titanium, rhubidium, strontium, sulfur, selenium, boron, nickel, arsenic, cobalt, silicon, lithium, aluminum, tin, and barium. Altogether, your body has 33 elements.

TABLE OF CHEMICAL ELEMENTS

Element	Symbol	Element	Symbol	Element	Symbol	Element	Symbol
Actinium	Ac	Erbium	Er	Mercury	Hg	Samarium	Sm
Aluminum	Al	Europium	Eu	Molybdenum	Mo	Scandium	Sc
Americium	Am	Fermium	Fm	Neodymium	Nd	Selenium	Se
Antimony	Sb	Fluorine	F	Neon	Ne	Silicon	Si
Argon	Ar	Francium	Fr	Neptunium	Np	Silver	Ag
Arsenic	As	Gadolinium	Gd	Nickel	Ni	Sodium	Na
Astatine	At	Gallium	Ga	Niobium	Nb	Strontium	Sr
Barium	Ba	Germanium	Ge	Nitrogen	N	Sulfur	S
Berkelium	Bk	Gold	Au	Nobelium	No	Tantalum	Ta
Beryllium	Be	Hafnium	Hf	Osmium	Os	Technetium	Tc
Bismuth	Bi	Helium	He	Oxygen	O	Tellurium	Te
Boron	B	Holmium	Ho	Palladium	Pd	Terbium	Tb
Bromine	Br	Hydrogen	H	Phosphorus	P	Thallium	Tl
Cadmium	Cd	Indium	In	Platinum	Pt	Thorium	Th
Calcium	Ca	Iodine	I	Plutonium	Pu	Thulium	Tm
Californium	Cf	Iridium	Ir	Polonium	Po	Tin	Sn
Carbon	C	Iron	Fe	Potassium	K	Titanium	Ti
Cerium	Ce	Krypton	Kr	Praseodymium	Pr	Tungsten	W
Cesium	Cs	Lanthanum	La	Promethium	Pm	Uranium	U
Chlorine	Cl	Lawrencium	Lw	Protactinium	Pa	Vanadium	V
Chromium	Cr	Lead	Pb	Radium	Ra	Xenon	Xe
Cobalt	Co	Lithium	Li	Radon	Rn	Ytterbium	Yb
Copper	Cu	Lutetium	Lu	Rhenium	Re	Yttrium	Y
Curium	Cm	Magnesium	Mg	Rhodium	Rh	Zinc	Zn
Dysprosium	Dy	Manganese	Mn	Rubidium	Rb	Zirconium	Zr
Einsteinium	E	Mendelevium	Mv	Ruthenium	Ru		

than writing out the whole name of the element. Chemists call the abbreviations *chemical symbols*. This name is inherited from alchemists who, as we learned, actually used symbols to refer to chemical elements.

Some abbreviations are simply the first letter, or first two letters, of the element's name; for example, *iodine* (I) or *nickel* (Ni). Other abbreviations are composed of the first letter and one other letter in the element's name; for example, *chlorine* (Cl) or *platinum* (Pt). These are easy to understand, but you may have noticed some abbreviations that are not made up of the letters in the element's name; for example, *gold* (Au). Why is this so? Because the letters of these abbreviations come from the Latin names of the elements. There is one other element whose abbreviation may puzzle you. It is *tungsten*, whose abbreviation is *W*. This is so because the proper name of

tungsten is *wolfram*, but it is a matter of custom to call this element tungsten in the United States. Here is a list of those elements whose abbreviations are derived from the Latin name:

ENGLISH NAME	LATIN NAME	ABBREVIATION
gold	aurum	Au
silver	argentum	Ag
copper	cuprum	Cu
iron	ferrum	Fe
lead	plumbum	Pb
tin	stannum	Sn
mercury	hydrargyrum	Hg
antimony	stibnium	Sb
potassium	kalium	K
sodium	natrium	Na

CHEMICAL COMPOUNDS

There are only 103 chemical elements,

What are chemical compounds?

but we know of almost a million other materials. What are these materials? They are combinations of two or more chemical elements and are called *chemical compounds*. To *compound* means "to put together." Chemical compounds are made by putting together chemical elements.

There are many compounds familiar to you. Water is one. Salt is another. Vinegar, sugar, aspirin, chalk, epsom salts, gasoline, lime, marble, rouge, washing soda and alcohol are still other compounds you know. Most of the materials you handle or use are chemical compounds or mixtures of chemical compounds.

Let us see of what elements a few familiar chemical compounds are made. (As you read the following, you may want to refer to the table of chemical elements.) Water is made of the elements *hydrogen* and *oxygen*. Table salt is made of *sodium* and *chlorine*. Chalk is made up of *calcium, carbon* and *oxygen*. Rouge is a combination of *iron* and *oxygen*. Alcohol is composed of *carbon, hydrogen* and *oxygen*.

When we say that water is made up of the elements hydrogen and oxygen, do we mean that if we mix together some hydrogen and some oxygen, we will have some water? No, for in order to make a chemical compound, we usually must use very special means of combining chemical elements. For example, if we were to put some oxygen in a jar that we previously emptied of air, and then were to add twice as great a volume of hydrogen, we would not be able to tell the contents of the jar from air simply by looking. But if we put into the jar two wires connected to an electric battery, and made a spark jump between the ends of the wires, we would cause an explosion within the jar. And

Water is a compound of oxygen and hydrogen.

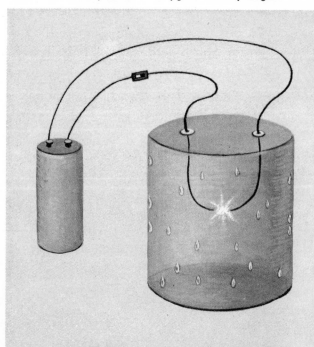

all around the sides of the jar would appear tiny drops of water. Since there was nothing at all in the jar until we put the hydrogen and oxygen into it, the water must have come from the combination of the two elements put into the jar. A chemist says that the hydrogen and oxygen *combined chemically* to form the compound called water.

An electric spark is not the only method of causing elements to combine into compounds; in fact, it is a rare method. One very common method is to heat the materials that we want to combine into compounds. Another method is to dissolve materials in water or other liquids, and then to mix the liquids, perhaps also heating them.

Since all compounds are made of elements, and since elements can be combined in so many different ways to make so many thousands of compounds, you can probably see the similarity between chemical elements and building blocks. It is because almost all the materials that we know of in the universe are made up of elements, compounds, or mixtures of these two, that elements are truly the building blocks of the universe.

Fill a tumbler half full of vinegar.

How can you make a compound? Crush a small piece of chalk. (If some kinds of chalk don't work, use crushed egg shell.) Drop the chalk into the vinegar. Soon you will see bubbles rising from the chalk. Where did they come from? They are made of *carbon dioxide* gas. This gas is composed of the elements carbon and oxygen combined into a single compound — the carbon dioxide.

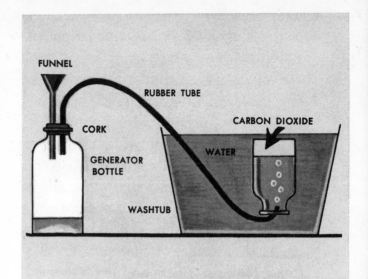

To make carbon dioxide, set up this apparatus. Place one-half inch of bicarbonate of soda in the generator bottle. Pour three ounces of vinegar into the funnel. To put the collection bottle in place, fill it with water, place your hand tightly over its mouth, turn it upside down under water, remove your hand.

The carbon and the oxygen, along with the element calcium, made up the chalk. The vinegar was able to remove the calcium from the chalk compound, leaving the carbon and oxygen to form the gas.

To combine two or three or more elements in order to make compounds is an unusual way of

In what other ways can we make compounds?

doing things in chemistry. Pure elements are difficult to obtain and are therefore expensive. Also, certain elements seem to be so eager to combine with others that it is difficult to keep them pure until we want to use them. Other elements seem so unwilling to combine that they require a great amount of trouble and expense to cause them to join with others. (Of course, chemical elements have no feelings, so they cannot really be "eager" or "unwilling," but to think

17

of them in this way helps us to understand their actions.)

By far the most common way of making chemical compounds is to bring together two or more compounds and exchange elements between them. For example, suppose we want to make some table salt. We learned that table salt is made up of the elements sodium and chlorine. We could make salt by simply bringing together some sodium and some chlorine. But if we actually tried this, we would find that we had problems on our hands. Chlorine is a very poisonous green gas, so it is difficult and dangerous to handle. Sodium is a metal that combines very easily with the oxygen of the air so that we would have a hard time to keep it pure until we could bring it into contact with the chlorine. And then, even if we solved these problems, there would be another,

for when the chlorine and sodium were brought into contact, they would begin to combine so energetically that an explosion would result.

There is, however, a very neat way in which we can combine sodium and chlorine. We could obtain two inexpensive, easy-to-handle powdered compounds called calcium chloride and sodium carbonate. Calcium chloride is made up of the elements calcium and chlorine, and sodium carbonate is made up of the elements sodium, carbon and oxygen. Now, both these compounds can be dissolved in water without combining with the water. Having dissolved the calcium chloride and the sodium carbonate in separate containers of water, we pour the water from both containers together. What happens? Again speaking figuratively, the sodium rushes into the arms of the chlorine, and the

SODIUM CARBONATE

CALCIUM CHLORIDE

DISSOLVE EACH IN SEPARATE CONTAINERS

By combining two elements, sodium, a pliable metal and chlorine, a poisonous gas, we get a harmless compound, sodium chloride.

COMBINE LIQUIDS FROM BOTH CONTAINERS

DISSOLVED TABLE SALT PLUS UNDISSOLVED CHALK

POUR LIQUID INTO PAN, LEAVING CHALK

HEAT PAN, EVAPORATING WATER, LEAVING ONLY SALT IN PAN

calcium joins hands with the carbon and oxygen.

The sodium and chlorine have formed table salt, but what have the rest of the elements made? The leftover elements are calcium carbon and oxygen. You may remember we learned that chalk is made up of calcium, carbon and oxygen — and chalk is exactly what the rest of our elements have combined to make. This chalk is in the form of very, very fine particles.

Chalk will not dissolve in water. So, the tiny particles of chalk simply settle to the bottom of the container of water. Let us wait for all the chalk to settle. Then we very carefully pour the water (and the salt dissolved in it) into a pan, leaving the chalk behind. We heat the pan until all the water boils away, and left on the bottom of the pan is pure *sodium chloride,* or table salt.

ATOMS AND MOLECULES

All matter is made up of extremely

What are atoms and molecules? small particles called *atoms*. Atoms are so small that no microscope, no matter how powerful, can enable you to see them. One hundred million atoms, side by side, would make a row only one inch long. We know of 103 kinds of atoms, each of a different size. Does the number *103* remind you of anything? You probably remember that there are 103 chemical elements. Each element is made up of just one kind of atom. We learned that an element is matter that cannot be divided into simpler parts. Now we can see that this is true because all of an element is made up of atoms of the same kind. No matter how much we divide up an element, we still have the same kind of atoms. (Of course, you may have heard of scientists who split, or smash, atoms. But when an atom is split, part of it becomes heat and light — and we learned that heat and light are not kinds of matter. So, we cannot properly say that splitting an atom divides it into simpler parts.)

We learned that elements are the simplest kinds of matter with which a chemist works. Now that we know what an atom is, we can add that an atom is the smallest unit of matter with which a chemist works.

Atoms sometimes exist by themselves, without connection to other atoms. Mostly, though, atoms form groups with other atoms. There may be only two atoms in a group or there may be hundreds. These groups of atoms are called *molecules*.

Sometimes two atoms of the same element join together to form a molecule. Chemists tell us that this two-atom molecule makes up most gases — hydrogen, oxygen and nitrogen, for example.

Usually, a molecule is made up of atoms of different elements. We learned that a chemical compound, too, is made up of different elements. Now, we can add that a compound is made up of molecules. When we learned that elements combine to make compounds, what we also meant was that atoms combine to make molecules.

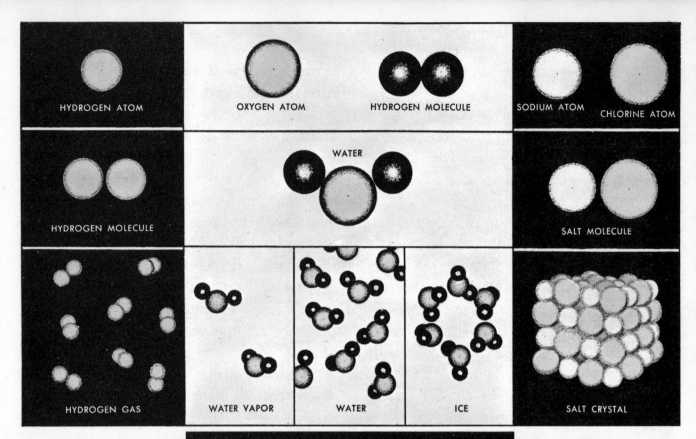

HYDROGEN ATOM   OXYGEN ATOM   HYDROGEN MOLECULE   SODIUM ATOM   CHLORINE ATOM

HYDROGEN MOLECULE   WATER   SALT MOLECULE

HYDROGEN GAS   WATER VAPOR   WATER   ICE   SALT CRYSTAL

Two hydrogen atoms combine to form a hydrogen molecule. Hydrogen gas is made of hydrogen molecules.

When two hydrogen atoms join an oxygen atom, a water molecule is formed. In water vapor, there is much room between the water molecules. In liquid water, they are closer together. In ice, they form shapely ice crystals.

When a sodium atom joins a chlorine atom, they form a sodium chloride molecule. These molecules join to form salt.

How do atoms combine? You probably know that a magnet will attract a piece of iron or steel, and that two magnets will attract each other. Atoms act like tiny magnets. They attract each other and join together. Since there are 103 different kinds of atoms, there are a vast number of ways in which they can join together. This is why there are so many compounds.

Not only can atoms join in so many different combinations, but also in many different patterns. Let us see some of these patterns. Suppose you could enlarge atoms until they became as large as marbles. With these large atoms, you could make models of molecules.

You might place two atoms side by side to form a model of a gas molecule.

You might add a third atom so as to form a triangular molecule. This would be the model of a water molecule. The oxygen atom would be larger than the two hydrogen atoms joined to it. If you wanted to add a fourth atom, you would place it on top of the other three, so as to form a little pyramid. In this case, the atoms would all have to be nearly the same size.

You might join all your atoms in a single row. Certain atoms actually do join in long rows, or chains, as the chemist calls them. You might join your atoms in the form of a circle. There really are molecules that are in the form of circles, or rings, as the chemist calls them. We shall learn more about chains and rings, because these arrangements of atoms make molecules of the greatest importance to man.

MIXTURES

What is a mixture? We have been talking about mixtures of many kinds of materials. In chemistry, we must clearly understand what a mixture is, so let us make one. We take a handful of the element *iron* in the form of filings; that is, in the form of powdered iron. Then we take a handful of the element *sulfur,* also in the form of a fine powder. We put enough of the two handfuls into a bottle so that the bottle is only half full. We cap the bottle and roll it around and around. Doing this thoroughly mixes the particles of iron and sulfur.

Is the mixture the same as a compound made up of iron and sulfur? No, because there are two important differences. To understand what these differences are, let us try two experiments.

First, let us see whether we can think of a way to separate the particles of iron and sulfur that make up our mixture. We might get a very fine pair of tweezers and try to pick all the particles of iron out of the mixture, thus leaving the sulfur behind. The trouble with this idea is that we couldn't get a pair of tweezers fine enough, nor probably have enough patience to pick out every single piece of iron. There is, however, an easy way to separate the iron and sulfur. We simply pull a magnet back and forth through our mixture. The iron particles cling to the magnet — the sulfur particles do not. Thus, we can separate the iron and sulfur, and no longer have a mixture.

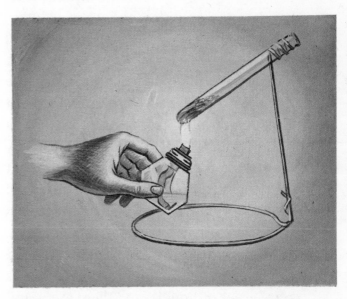

Sulphur and iron joined in a compound do change.

Can we separate a compound of iron and sulfur in the same way? Let us see. We make the iron and sulfur mixture again. Now we put the mixture into a small porcelain crucible, or a test tube. We then heat the tube. At the proper temperature, the mixture begins to glow and give off heat, as if it were burning. When the glowing stops and the tube cools, let us dump out the contents and examine it closely.

Sulphur and iron joined in a mixture stay unchanged.

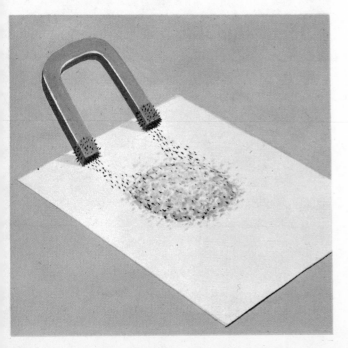

21

Out of the tube comes a lump made up of black crystals. We no longer see particles of either iron or sulfur. If we bring a magnet close to the lump, nothing clings to the magnet. What happened to the particles of iron and sulfur that went into the mixture? They combined chemically to form the crystals that are a compound called *iron sulfide*. Can we separate iron sulfide into iron and sulfur? Yes, but doing so will be a long and complicated process in which we use many compounds and several chemical operations.

Now we can see what is the first difference between a mixture and a compound:

How do mixtures and compounds differ?

The materials that make up a mixture remain unchanged in the mixture; but the materials that go into making a compound change completely as they form the compound. We learned about a very dramatic change of this kind when we saw how two gases, hydrogen and oxygen, combine to form a liquid, water. There are thousands of solid compounds, part of whose ingredients are gases or liquids, and there are liquid compounds whose ingredients are solids or gases.

When we were making the mixture of iron filings and sulfur powder, we could have mixed together as much or as little of each of these ingredients as we wished. We could have used half iron and half sulfur or ten times as much of one as the other.

In making a compound we do not have a free choice of how much of each ingredient we will have in the compound. In iron sulfide there is combined just one part of iron with one part of sulfur — no more and no less. If we had used more iron than sulfur, the extra iron would have been left over. (We may not have been able to see the extra iron just by looking, but if we had ground up the lump of iron sulfide and then pulled a magnet through the powder, we could have removed the *extra* iron, but not the iron that combined with the sulfur to make iron sulfide.)

Now we know the second difference between a mixture and a compound: A mixture can be made up of ingredients in any amounts, but a compound is made up of ingredients in only certain fixed amounts that are always the same.

RAIN

FRESH WATER

OCEAN

There is one kind of mixture that does

When is a mixture not a mixture? not act like other mixtures. Let us make it. First we take a glass of water into which we place a teaspoon of table salt. Stir the water with a spoon. What happens to the salt? It disappears. A chemist says that the salt *dissolves*. The water and the dissolved salt together make up a solution.

Let us pour the solution from the glass into a pan and put the pan on a lighted stove. We let the solution boil until all of the water goes up in steam. On the bottom of the pan is the same amount of salt as we dissolved in the glassful of water.

Insofar as the solution can be made up

How is a solution and mixture alike and different, too? of ingredients in varying amounts, it is like a mixture.

Also, the ease with which we separated the ingredients shows that they were not chemically combined to form a compound. In this way, too, a solution is like a mixture. But when the salt was dissolved in the water, we could not see separate parts of salt and water, for the salt had taken on an entirely new form. In this way the solution is different from a mixture.

There is more than one kind of solution. Not only can solids (like salt) be dissolved in liquids (like water), but liquids can be dissolved in other liquids, and gases can be dissolved in liquids. We have learned that the bubbles in soda water are carbon dioxide gas. We see bubbles only when the carbon dioxide begins to separate from the water in which it was dissolved.

Solutions are very important in chem-

How do the chemists form new compounds? istry. By dissolving materials —

compounds and elements — in liquids, the chemist has his chief way of bringing materials together to form new

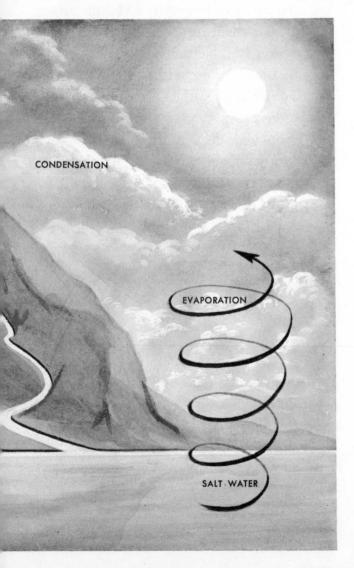

CONDENSATION

EVAPORATION

SALT WATER

Nature is continually manufacturing fresh and salt water. The sun's heat evaporates water from the sea to form clouds that are made up of fresh-water droplets. Rain from the clouds runs through the ground and dissolves salt compounds. Streams and rivers carry the dissolved salts to the sea where the salt collects, and the sea becomes saltier. The sun evaporates more sea water as the process continues.

compounds. Do you remember that when we were learning about compounds, we found how to make table salt (sodium chloride) from two other compounds called calcium chloride and sodium carbonate? These latter two were powdered. If we simply mixed the powders together, kept them dry and left them alone, nothing would have happened. But we dissolved the powders in water. Then the compounds easily acted to form new compounds. In the chemical industry, dissolving compounds in liquids is probably the main way of bringing materials together to make new materials.

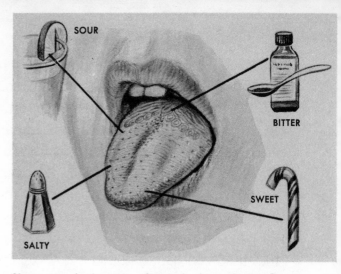

Shown are the location of taste buds on the tongue.

Solutions are important to us when we eat. Our tongues have certain areas in which there are small organs called *taste buds*. Different taste buds give us different taste sensations. There are taste buds for sweet, sour, salty and bitter tastes. We do not know exactly how taste buds work, but we do know that tasting is some kind of chemical

How do we taste things?

action. How do we know this? Because we can taste only those materials that dissolve in liquids. Saliva is one liquid that dissolves some of our food materials; water is another.

If you want to prove that a material must be dissolved in order to be tasted, try to taste a clean spoon or the edge of a clean plate. Neither silver nor china can dissolve in your saliva. That is why you cannot taste either of them. Put a dry soda cracker in your mouth. At first, you will taste nothing. In a few seconds, your saliva will begin to dissolve the cracker, and you will taste it.

Some Interesting Elements

Each of the 103 chemical elements has an interesting story. Elements have different colors. Some are metals, some are crystals, some are liquids and some are gases. Elements are obtained in many different ways, and elements have many interesting uses. Let us look closely at a few of them.

We have learned that alchemists discovered several chemical elements, but we know about the actual discovery of only one of these elements. In 1669, a German alchemist, Hennig Brand,

Which element is noted for glowing in the dark, and how was it found?

was trying to make gold from cheaper materials. Because gold was considered to be the most perfect metal, alchemists called it a "noble" metal. Brand reasoned that nothing could be more noble than the human body and materials connected with it. So, perhaps, it would be possible to change something connected with the noble human body into the noble metal, gold.

With this idea in mind, Brand mixed together some human urine and sand, and heated them in an oven. We do not know why he chose sand, but it was not unusual for alchemists to heat together any odd combination of materials that came to mind. When taken from the cooled oven, Brand's mixture glowed strongly in the dark. Brand had not, of course, made gold, but he had made a soft, whitish, waxy material. This material had been in a compound dissolved in the urine, although Brand did not know this. He named the glowing material *phosphorus*, which is Greek for the words "I bear light." Phosphorus turned out to be an element — it could not be divided into simpler materials.

A century and a half after the discovery of this element, it was found that phosphorus mixed with other materials would catch fire when rubbed. This mixture was used to make tips for matches. Unfortunately, since phosphorus is very poisonous, many people who worked in match factories died from breathing the vapor of heated phosphorus. But fortunately, in 1845, another kind of phosphorus—red phosphorus—was discovered. It is not poisonous and eventually, all countries passed laws that

At the left is an alchemist's oven; right, Brand discovers phosphorus.

banned the use of white phosphorus in the manufacture of matches.

Phosphorus is very important to the

Why is phosphorus useful to humans?

proper growth of the human body, especially for the development of healthy bones and teeth. Phosphorus is also needed to keep nerves and muscles healthy. The phosphorus in our bodies is combined with other chemical elements and is not at all poisonous. We can get enough phosphorus for good health from a balanced diet, especially from milk. Plants, too, need phosphorus, and this element is a part of most fertilizers.

Sometimes chemists need large amounts of phosphorus. To get it, they put burned bones or a certain kind of rock, called phosphate rock, into a furnace along with sand and coke. In both the bones and rock there are compounds containing much phosphorus. This mixture is heated, and large amounts of phosphorus are obtained as a result of this process.

The most abundant element on earth

What is the most abundant element in the earth's crust?

is a colorless, odorless, tasteless gas that is important to you every moment of your life. This element is *oxygen*. One-fifth of the weight

26

The French chemist Antoine Lavoisier showed that when oxygen combines *slowly* with iron or certain other metals, rusting takes place, and when oxygen combines *rapidly* with the elements that make up wood, for example, burning occurs. This sort of rapid combining of oxygen with a substance is *combustion*.

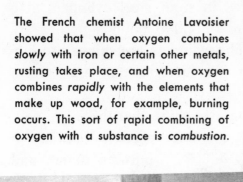

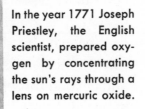

In the year 1771 Joseph Priestley, the English scientist, prepared oxygen by concentrating the sun's rays through a lens on mercuric oxide.

of the atmosphere and nine-tenths of the weight of all the earth's water is oxygen. Nearly half of the weight of the earth's rocky crust and one-third of the weight of the deeper rocks is oxygen. And oxygen makes up two-thirds of your body and the tissues of most other living things.

In the late fifteenth century, the Italian scientist and artist Leonardo da Vinci wrote that the atmosphere contained two different gases. Two hundred years later, an Englishman, John Mayow, discovered that one of the gases in air caused iron to rust and was

important to breathing. Sixty years later another Englishman, Stephen Hales, actually obtained some oxygen by heating a compound called saltpeter. Hales, like the alchemists, called all gases "air," and so he never knew he discovered a new gas. Exactly forty years later, a Swedish apothecary, Karl Wilhelm Scheele, produced some pure oxygen. He realized that he had discovered a new gas, but he did not have any way of telling the scientific world about it. Three years later, Joseph Priestley, an English clergyman, also produced pure oxygen. He immediately told his fellow scientists about his accomplishment. Scheele did not publish his results until three years after Priestley reported his discovery. For this reason, Priestley was for a long time given credit as the discoverer of oxygen, but now we say that both men deserve equal credit as the discoverers of this important element.

Oxygen is very useful in a chemical laboratory and also in industry. If we want just a little oxygen we have several ways of obtaining it. We might get oxygen the way Priestley did; that is, we could heat a compound called mercuric oxide. This compound is a reddish powder that is composed of the elements mercury and oxygen. Gently heating mercuric oxide will cause the oxygen to separate from the mercury. There are a few other compounds from which we could get oxygen by heating them.

How can we get oxygen?

Still another way to get small amounts of oxygen is to run an electric current through water. We learned that water is composed of hydrogen and oxygen. The electric current separates the atoms of the water molecule, and water changes into hydrogen and oxygen.

In industry, much larger amounts of oxygen are needed than can be conveniently obtained by the methods described above. To obtain large amounts of oxygen, we turn to the air, which is one-fifth oxygen. This portion of oxygen is not combined with any other element. To separate the oxygen from the eight other gases that normally make up the atmosphere, air is put into containers under very great pressure. As a result the air becomes liquid and very cold. Then the pressure is gradually released and the liquid air is allowed to slowly warm up. As the warming takes place, each of the gases that make up the air boils off at a different temperature. Oxygen boils off at 297 degrees below zero Fahrenheit. As the oxygen boils off it is caught in other containers, and then is stored in stout steel cylinders at a pressure of 2,000 pounds per square inch. The cylinders are shipped to laboratories or factories that use oxygen.

Did you ever think that there is a connection between a burning match and a rusting nail? Well, there is. When a match burns, oxygen is *rapidly* combining with some of the elements that make up the wood of the match. When a nail rusts, oxygen is *slowly* combining with the iron of the nail. In both these cases, the combining oxygen is producing heat. It is easy to tell that a burning match gives off heat; it is difficult to measure the heat given off by a rusting nail, but it can be done. This sort of combination of oxygen with other kinds of matter is called *combustion*.

How is oxygen used by the human body?

When you breathe air into your lungs, some of the air is taken into the blood and carried through the arteries to food materials stored in the muscles and other tissues. Here the oxygen combines with the food materials and produces heat to warm your body and energy to move your muscles. This combination of oxygen with the food materials is really slow combustion, just like the rusting of a nail. Since your heart must continue to beat as long as you are alive, you have a continuous need for energy; so you must continuously burn food materials in your tissues to keep your heart beating. When a human being is deprived of air for even a few minutes — as, for example, in drowning — his heart cannot get the oxygen it needs for energy, and the heart stops beating. Thus, oxygen is not only the most abundant element, but it is also the most important to living beings.

Everyone has seen some form of the element carbon. A piece of coal, a burned match, the lead of a lead-pencil, a diamond, and soot from a burning candle — all these are forms of the element carbon. A diamond is the hardest natural material known. (Up until very recently, diamond was the hardest, but now chemists have made a compound of the elements carbon and boron that is harder than diamond.) A diamond is so hard because the carbon atoms that make up the diamond are packed very closely together.

Why are diamonds so hard?

Everyone knows that diamonds are valuable, and one that is entirely transparent, with no elements mixed into it to color it, is very rare. The closely-packed atoms of a diamond have a remarkable effect on light that passes through the diamond. They cause the light to come out of the diamond in bright sparkles of all the colors of the rainbow. Because of this, we say that a diamond has *fire* and *luster,* and these two qualities are what make diamonds so highly prized as jewels.

Some diamonds are black or dark brown. These diamonds are used in industry to cut, grind or drill hard metals, such as steel.

Until recently, all diamonds were mined from the earth. But in 1955, an American company began to manufacture diamonds. These diamonds are the black kind. The manufacturing process is a secret, but we can make a pretty

Charcoal is made out of wood.

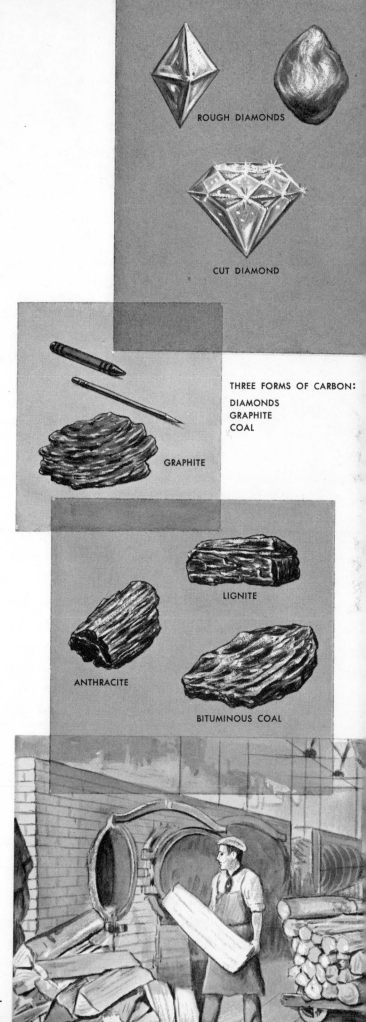

ROUGH DIAMONDS

CUT DIAMOND

THREE FORMS OF CARBON:
DIAMONDS
GRAPHITE
COAL

GRAPHITE

LIGNITE

ANTHRACITE

BITUMINOUS COAL

During the "coal age," about 250 million years ago, huge tree-ferns and giant mosses flourished in the hot, humid weather. These plants toppled to the ground when they died and sank in the mud, forming the basis for coal deposits.

good guess at how it is done. In 1887, a French chemist named Henri Moissan dissolved some charcoal (a form of carbon) in molten iron. He plunged the iron into water. The cooling iron exerted tremendous pressure on the dissolved carbon, and the carbon formed tiny diamonds. The modern process, too, uses some kind of great pressure to squeeze the carbon atoms as close together as they are found in diamonds.

The lead in a lead pencil is not really **What causes the "writing" when you write with a lead pencil?** made of the element lead — it is a form of carbon called *graphite*. (Once upon a time, lead pencils actually did have thin rods of lead in them.) The carbon atoms in graphite are connected together in the form of thin sheets. These sheets, layer upon layer, easily slide over one another. This is why part of the graphite of a pencil so easily slides off to leave a line on the paper upon which we are writing. Powdered graphite is used instead of oil to help parts of machines to slide easily over one another.

In the third kind of carbon, represented **How is charcoal made?** by charcoal and carbon black, the atoms are arranged in tiny interlocking flakes. This is called *amorphous* carbon. Charcoal is made by burning wood in an insufficient supply of air. Carbon black is made by burning natural gas under like conditions. Burning in this manner gets rid of the other materials that make up wood and natural gas, and leaves behind nearly pure carbon.

Carbon black has many uses. You are looking at one of them right now.

Carbon black mixed with the proper oils makes printer's ink. Also, the ink on black typewriter ribbons and the surface of black carbon paper contain carbon black. Carbon black is added to rubber to increase its toughness and wearing qualities. Every automobile tire contains several pounds of carbon black.

Coal is almost all carbon. *Bituminous,* or soft, coal is eighty-eight per cent carbon, while *anthracite,* or hard, coal is ninety-five percent carbon. You probably know that all coal is mined, but how did the coal happen to be in the ground? About 250 million years ago, the climate all over the world, except in the most northern parts, was warm and damp. It rained much, and it was always as warm as it

Where did coal come from? How was it formed?

now is in tropical regions. Swamps covered much of the surface of the earth. Among the many plants that grew in abundance in the warm, wet climate were some called tree-ferns. They looked like huge ferns, some being a hundred feet tall. There were no trees in the world at this time. The tree-ferns were not made of wood, but of a softer material. However, like wood, this material was largely carbon. The trunks of tree-ferns were green and scaly, and at their tops grew fronds like those on fern plants today.

Tree-ferns grew in great numbers, making forests in all parts of the world. The forests were so thick and the tree-ferns grew so close together that no sunlight could ever shine through the fern tops to the ground beneath.

When the tree-ferns died, they fell into the swamps in which they were standing and sank into the mud. More

The pressure of layers of tree-ferns and mud as well as the earth's folding crust changed plants to coal beds.

Thousands of compounds from vanilla flavoring and medicine to perfume and explosives are made out of coal tar by chemists.

tree-ferns died and fell upon those that were already buried. More mud covered the newly-fallen plants. The weight of the fallen tree-ferns and the mud pressed heavily upon those that were buried deeply. Water and other liquids were pressed out of the tree-fern trunks. Later, tremendous pressure of the earth's folding crust further squeezed the remains of the buried plants. This process took tens of millions of years, and at its end, practically nothing was left of the buried tree-ferns but large masses of carbon. These masses are the coal beds that we mine for coal today.

Coal has been found in thirty-seven of the fifty United States. Last year, more than a half million tons were mined. Most of this coal was burned to provide heat for homes and power for factories. But about one-quarter of all the coal mined was used to make thousands of different kinds of plastics, dyes, varnishes and lacquers, perfumes, synthetic rubber, explosives and drugs. How was this done?

How are several useful materials obtained from coal?

To obtain material from coal to make all the things we have just listed, the coal is placed into large ovens, called by-product ovens, from which all air is excluded. The coal is then heated red-hot. Ordinarily, at this heat, coal burns, but the coal in by-product ovens cannot burn. Why not? Because, as we learned, burning is the rapid combination of oxygen with another material. Since air is excluded from the by-product ovens, there is no oxygen to combine with the coal. Instead of burning, the heated coal separates into the materials from which it is made. Chief among these are coal gas, tar, coke and a compound called ammonium sulfate. The coal gas may be piped away from the by-product ovens and sold to consumers for heating their homes or cooking their food. The ammonium sulfate is used to make fertilizer. The coke is used by iron and steel mills in the process of smelting.

The materials in coal tar are a chemist's delight. By separating coal tar into its principal compounds — benzene, toluene, phenol, anthracene and naphthalene — the chemist can make thousands of compounds ranging from vanilla flavoring and medicine to perfume and TNT.

There can be no argument about the fact that if it had not been for *iron*, we would never have been able to build the great industries that have made modern civilization possible. Iron's strength, hardness and springy

What is the most important element in modern times?

The Bessemer process for converting pig iron into steel takes about fifteen minutes.

Metal is separated from ore in blast furnaces.

DOUBLE BELL AND HOPPER

HOT GASES TO BLAST STOVES

IRON ORE, COKE AND LIME

PIPE FOR HOT AIR BLAST

MOLTEN SLAG AND IRON

SLAG OUTLET

IRON OUTLET

toughness have made possible the construction of skyscraper frames, ocean liners, battleships, railroads, automobiles, typewriters, tanks and most of the machines and machine tools that have given us our industrial civilization.

In 4000 B.C., Egyptian pharaohs valued iron more highly than gold. At that time, the only iron available came from rare pieces that fell to earth as meteorites. It was not until 1500 B.C. that anyone learned to produce iron in fairly large quantities. At this time, a people of Asia Minor, the Hittites, learned how to obtain iron from iron ore. They used the iron to make swords, spears, helmets and shields. With these weapons they were very successful in war, because their enemies had bronze weapons that were softer than iron. Almost a thousand years more passed before most of the peoples who lived on the shore of the Mediterranean Sea had learned to obtain and use iron. When Julius Caesar landed in Britain, in 55 B.C., he found the people making iron.

Iron is the fourth most abundant element in the earth's crust, where it makes up one-twentieth of the total of all elements. However, if many scientists are correct in their belief that the earth's core (about 4,300 miles in diameter) is largely iron, then iron, and not oxygen, is the earth's most abundant element.

In the earth's crust, iron is in the form of iron ore. This ore consists of iron combined with oxygen. In order to get the iron in a form we can use, we must

How do we put iron in a form so that it can be used by man?

separate it from the oxygen. The process of doing this is called *smelting*. In general, smelting is done by heating iron ore mixed with charcoal or coke. Charcoal and coke both are forms of the chemical element, carbon. When iron ore and carbon are very hot, the atoms of oxygen become disconnected from the iron and connect with the carbon. This leaves iron in the form of the metal that is so familiar to us. What makes this process so easily workable is due to the fact that when the oxygen combines with the carbon, the compound that is formed is a gas that is driven off by the heat into the atmosphere. Thus, we do not have to worry about separating the carbon-and-oxygen compound from the iron we have obtained.

In the iron industry, smelting is done in huge ovens called *blast furnaces*. These furnaces are tall steel cylinders lined with brick, ten or twelve stories high. A fire is built in the bottom of the blast furnace, and iron ore and coke are dumped into the top of the furnace. At the bottom, encircling the furnace, is a ring of pipes. Through these pipes a strong blast of air is continually blown into the furnace in order to make the fire inside very hot. It is this blast of air that gives the blast furnace its name. In iron smelting plants, eight or ten blast furnaces are built next to each other in a double row. During the day, great columns of smoke pour out of the tops of the furnaces, while at night their fires light up the sky with a red glow.

The smelted iron collects at the bottom of the furnace. The iron is molten and runs as easily as water. When enough iron has collected, a hole is

opened on the side at the bottom of the furnace. From this hole, the molten iron flows out of the furnace in a fiery stream. The iron flows into molds lined with sand. When the iron has cooled, it is in the shape of long heavy bars called "pigs," and the iron is thus called "pig iron." Most blast furnaces produce 400 to 500 tons of iron a day, and some can produce as much as 1,000 tons.

Pig iron is hard and strong, but it is brittle, which means that it is easily broken by a blow. If our machines were made of pig iron, we would continually have to be repairing their broken parts. What we need is a kind of iron that is tough as well as hard. The two main kinds of tough iron are called *wrought iron* and *steel*.

If we add just the right amount of car-

How is steel made?

bon to iron, we get steel. This kind of iron is not only tough, but it can be made very hard. Steel is easily shaped by casting, rolling, drawing and hammering. It has great resistance to breaking under pull. An excellent grade of steel was manufactured at Damascus and at Toledo in Spain during the Middle Ages. Swords manufactured in these two cities were highly prized for the

springiness and hardness of the steel. The point of one of these swords could be bent all the way around to the hilt without breaking the blade. Armor, too, was made of steel.

One process for making steel uses a furnace called a *Bessemer converter*. It converts iron to steel, and was invented by Henry Bessemer. This furnace is a pear-shaped vessel, twelve to fifteen feet high, constructed of iron plates and lined with brick. It is hung by two thick, hollow iron rods attached to its sides at half its height, so that it can be tipped on its side. The brick lining is heated white-hot by a coal or oil fire. The converter is turned on its side and ten to twenty-five tons of molten pig iron are poured into it. It is brought back to an upright position and 20,000 cubic feet of air per minute are forced through one of the hollow supporting rods. The air enters the converter through the bottom and rushes upward through the molten iron. This burns out the impurities in the iron. The action is spectacular as a great torch of flame shoots out of the mouth of the converter with a roar and a shower of sparks. Within ten to twenty minutes the flame dies out. The converter is again turned on its side and a mixture

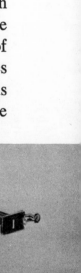

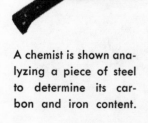

A chemist is shown analyzing a piece of steel to determine its carbon and iron content.

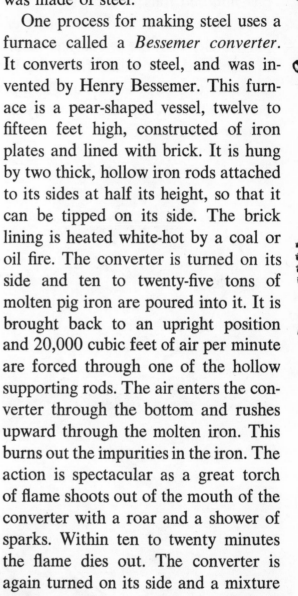

of the elements manganese and carbon is put into the converter. This mixture, called *spiegeleisen*, changes the iron to steel. A modern converter can produce one hundred tons of steel in an hour.

A modern steel and iron plant employs many chemists to analyze samples of steel and iron taken from the furnaces. In this way the steel and iron can be made to have the proper purity and other needed qualities.

Organic Chemistry

What is organic chemistry and carbon chemistry?

In the year 1828, a young German chemist, Friedrich Wöhler, made in his laboratory a compound called *urea*. The news of this accomplishment astounded the scientific world. Urea had been known as a compound made by human kidneys and as one of the waste products of the body. What, then, was so remarkable about Wöhler's making urea in a labo-

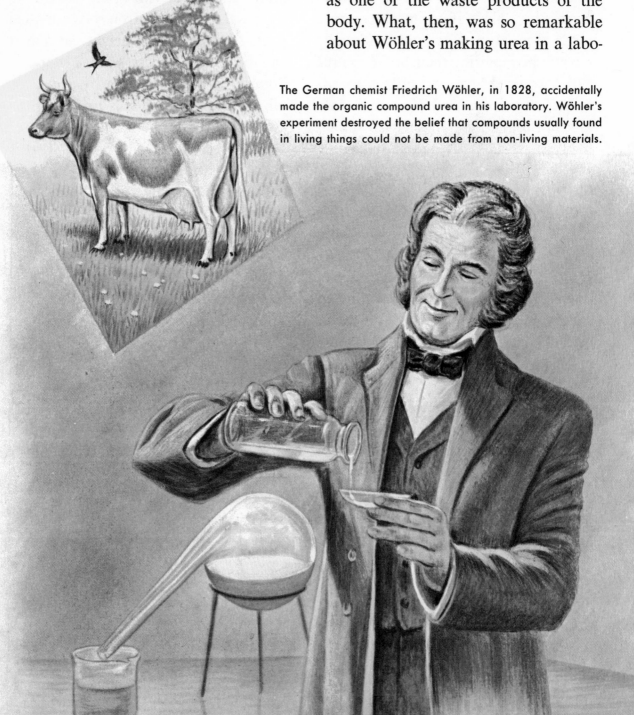

The German chemist Friedrich Wöhler, in 1828, accidentally made the organic compound urea in his laboratory. Wöhler's experiment destroyed the belief that compounds usually found in living things could not be made from non-living materials.

ratory? Before Wöhler's accomplishment, it had been believed that any of the materials of a living thing — plant or animal — or any of the products of these living things, contained an ingredient called a "vital spirit." This vital spirit was believed to be forever beyond man's grasp, and without it he could never reproduce any of the materials of which living things are made. By making urea in a laboratory, Wöhler had, at one stroke, destroyed the vital spirit theory.

As soon as the meaning of Wöhler's success was understood, scientists realized that the whole great field of the chemistry of living things had been opened. This new field of chemistry soon had two names: *organic chemistry* and *carbon chemistry*.

Since this field of chemistry had to do with the chemistry of living things — that is, living *organisms* — it is not hard to see where the name "organic chemistry" came from.

As knowledge of the field of organic chemistry grew, it was found that almost all of the tens of thousands of compounds found in living organisms not only contained carbon, but also depended on the properties of carbon. So the new field was also called *carbon chemistry*.

Since Wöhler's discovery, organic **How did a dream solve an important chemical problem?** chemists have studied more than 700,000 carbon compounds. It is now clear that carbon can form more compounds than any other element. Why? Because carbon

Carbon compounds: rubber, cotton, wood, sugar, wool.

atoms can connect to each other in long chains and in rings. Most molecules have only a few atoms, but carbon atom chains may contain hundreds of atoms. Usually, organic compounds contain hundreds of atoms. Carbon can combine with most other elements. There are more carbon compounds than all other chemical compounds put together. Wood, paper, wool, nylon, rubber, oil, alcohol, soap, fat and plastics are carbon compounds or mixtures of carbon compounds. Many compounds, called *hydrocarbons*, are composed only of carbon and hydrogen. Among them are natural gas, fuel oil, gasoline and paraffin. Other compounds, made up of carbon, hydrogen and oxygen, are called *carbohydrates*.

In working with these compounds, the organic chemist takes apart linkings of carbon chains and puts them together in different combinations. To understand what the organic chemist is doing, you might picture a carbon atom as a tiny ball with four sharp hooks projecting from it at opposite points. These hooks can link up with the hooks on other carbon atoms or the atoms of other elements — hydrogen, for example. To understand just how carbon atoms are linked to each other or to other atoms requires many years of study by the organic chemist. Today, most chemists are organic chemists.

We learned that one way in which carbon atoms can link up is in rings. In the early days of organic chemistry, it was found that a large number of hydrocarbons had six carbon atoms joined in a ring. Organic chemists soon found they had a difficult problem when

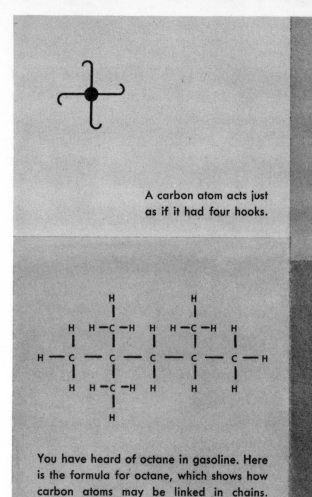

A carbon atom acts just as if it had four hooks.

You have heard of octane in gasoline. Here is the formula for octane, which shows how carbon atoms may be linked in chains.

Kekulé's dream solved the carbon ring linkage riddle.

they tried to figure out just how the carbon atoms formed the ring. Two of the connecting "hooks" on each carbon atom were used in joining it to the carbon atoms on each side of it. One more "hook" on each carbon atom was used to join some other atom to the ring, perhaps a hydrogen atom. But what was done with the other "hook"? If chemists considered it to be connected in a double connection to neighboring carbon atoms, they ended up with too many connections. They could not just consider it to be waving around empty, because all the "hooks" on an atom in a compound must be connected.

One afternoon, a German chemist, Friedrich Kekulé, who was working on the problem of the carbon ring linkage,

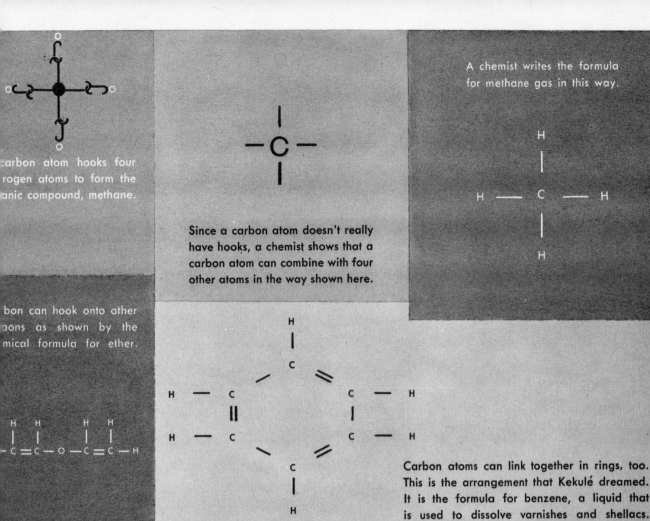

A carbon atom hooks four hydrogen atoms to form the organic compound, methane.

Since a carbon atom doesn't really have hooks, a chemist shows that a carbon atom can combine with four other atoms in the way shown here.

A chemist writes the formula for methane gas in this way.

Carbon can hook onto other carbons as shown by the chemical formula for ether.

Carbon atoms can link together in rings, too. This is the arrangement that Kekulé dreamed. It is the formula for benzene, a liquid that is used to dissolve varnishes and shellacs.

dozed off in a chair before the fireplace. Kekulé dreamed that he saw the six carbon atoms dancing around among the flames in his fireplace. Suddenly, the dancing atoms formed a ring with every "hook" used in just the right way. Kekulé remembered his dream when he awoke, and the problem of the six-atom ring was solved. The arrangement Kekulé dreamed is shown on this page.

Here you can see carbon combining in many ways. The chemical formula shown above is for aspirin.

What do plants provide us with?

There is an old saying that all flesh is grass. This means that all animals get their flesh either by eating plants or by eating other animals that eat plants. Cows and sheep eat grass. In their bodies, the grass eventually becomes flesh. Cougars do not eat grass, but they do eat cows and sheep. In the body of the cougar, the cow and sheep flesh becomes cougar flesh. Thus, indirectly, cougar flesh comes from grass. Aphids eat the juices of rosebushes. Praying mantises eat aphids. Robins eat praying mantises. Hawks eat rob-

39

"FLESH IS GRASS"

CAT EATS BIRD,
THAT FEEDS ON INSECTS,
WHICH LIVE ON PLANTS.

bins. Thus, hawk flesh was once rose-bush juice. Human beings maintain the flesh on their bodies by eating both animal flesh and plants. In short, then, every animal is dependent on plants for food.

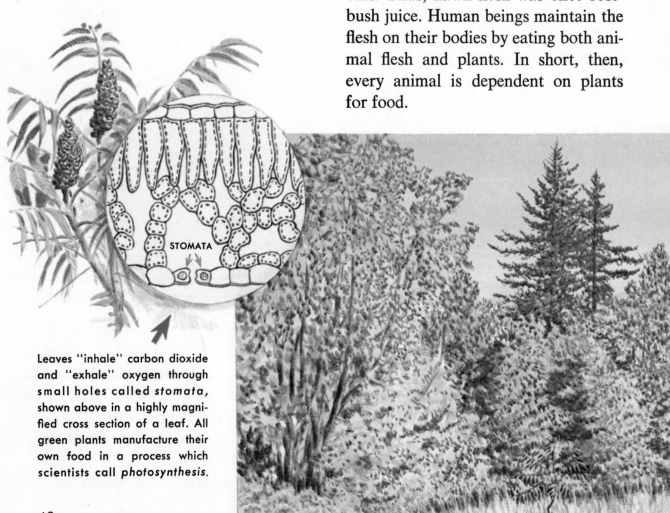

STOMATA

Leaves "inhale" carbon dioxide and "exhale" oxygen through small holes called *stomata*, shown above in a highly magnified cross section of a leaf. All green plants manufacture their own food in a process which scientists call *photosynthesis*.

Most plants — the green plants —

Where do plants get their food?

manufacture their own food in a wonderful chemical factory. The green plant uses two raw materials: water from the soil and carbon dioxide gas from the air. To do the work of changing these two raw materials into food, the green plant needs energy — just as any chemical factory needs energy. The plant gets the needed energy from sunlight.

What kind of food does a green plant make from carbon dioxide and water? It makes a kind of sugar called *glucose*. If you were to eat some glucose you would find that it does not taste as sweet as the sugar you put on your cereal.

Right after a plant makes glucose in its leaves, the plant changes the glucose to starch. The starch, which is dissolved in water, is carried by the plant through tiny tubes in its stem to the root where the starch is stored.

In addition to making starch, a green plant makes *cellulose*, the main constituent of wood. Why is it that only green plants can make glucose, starch and cellulose? Because only green plants contain a carbon compound called *chlorophyll*. In fact, it is the green color of chlorophyll that makes plants green. The process in which a green plant uses water, carbon dioxide and chlorophyll to make glucose in the presence of sunlight is called *photosynthesis*. This word means "put together with the help of light."

1
2
3

Pin a strip of tinfoil or black cloth across the upper surface of some leaves of a house plant. A geranium is a good plant to use. Have each strip cover about a third of the leaf. Place the plant in a sunny window for two or three days. Cut the partly-covered leaves from the plant. Remove the tinfoil or cloth. Soak the leaves overnight in alcohol. The next day, take the leaves out of the alcohol. With a medicine dropper, drop iodine on both parts of the leaves that were covered and the parts that were not. The parts that were not covered will turn purple or dark blue. This color proves that starch is present.

PHOTOSYNTHESIS

SUNLIGHT SUPPLIES ENERGY

CARBON DIOXIDE IS ABSORBED FROM THE AIR

OXYGEN GIVEN OFF AS WASTE

WATER TAKEN IN THROUGH THE ROOTS RISES THROUGH THE STEM

Chlorophyll plays a very interesting role in the process of photosynthesis. In a green plant, six molecules of carbon dioxide combine with six molecules of water and 673,000 calories of energy from sunlight to make one molecule of glucose and six molecules of oxygen. If the chlorophyll is not present, the sunlight will not cause the water and carbon dioxide to combine. Yet the chlorophyll does not become part of the glucose. Evidently, then, the chlorophyll helps the water and carbon dioxide become glucose, but the chlorophyll itself remains unchanged. Chemists know about many compounds that act this way. Such compounds are called *catalysts*. This term comes from the Greek words which mean "entirely loose" and refers to the fact that the catalyst is entirely loose from the compounds it helps to combine.

Chlorophyll: What does it do?

The chemical factory within a plant does not end its work with the making of glucose, starch and cellulose. The water that enters the plant through the roots brings with it many dissolved chemical compounds called *minerals*. The plant combines these minerals with starch to make fats, oils and proteins. You have probably noticed how oily peanuts are. Lima beans and kidney beans contain much protein. And nuts contain fat.

Did you ever stop to wonder why, during all the millions of years that animals have been living on earth, all the oxygen in the air was not long ago all breathed up? We just learned the answer to this question when we learned that the process of photosynthesis not only results in the manufacture of glucose, but also oxygen. So, it is the activity of plants that continually renews the oxygen in the air. But this is not the end of this wonderful arrangement. We learned that we slowly burn food materials in our tissues. These stored food materials are carbon compounds. When oxygen combines with these compounds, water and carbon dioxide gas are formed. When we exhale a breath from our lungs, it is made up partly of water and carbon dioxide. By breathing out carbon dioxide into the air, we make this gas available to plants for the process of photosynthesis.

What is the oxygen-carbon dioxide cycle?

Here we have a remarkable circular

HOW CAN YOU USE A CATALYST?

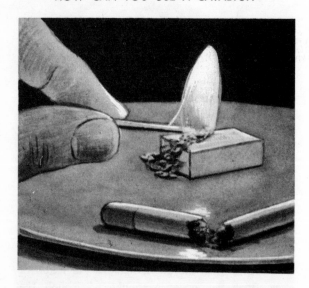

Place a lump of sugar in a saucer. Try to light it with a match. Can you make the sugar catch fire? No. Now rub the lump of sugar in an ashtray, so that the sugar picks up some cigarette or cigar ashes. Place a lighted match against the sugar where it is smeared with ash. Does it catch fire now? Answer: Yes. Did the ash act as a catalyst? Answer: Yes.

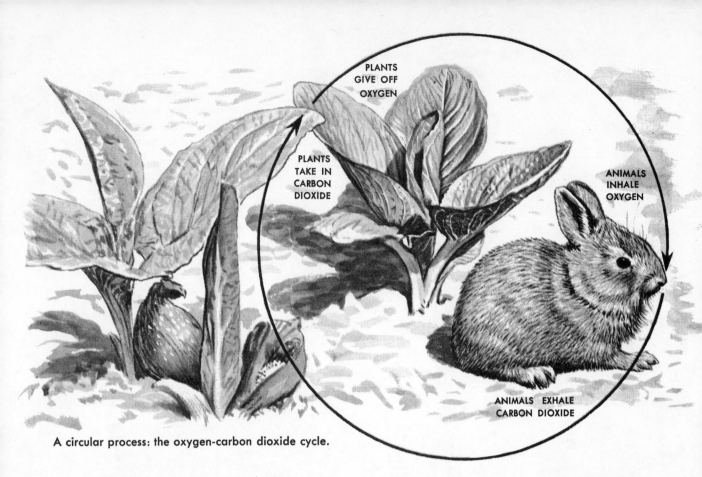

PLANTS
GIVE OFF
OXYGEN

PLANTS
TAKE IN
CARBON
DIOXIDE

ANIMALS
INHALE
OXYGEN

ANIMALS EXHALE
CARBON DIOXIDE

A circular process: the oxygen-carbon dioxide cycle.

arrangement: animals use oxygen and make carbon dioxide, while plants use that carbon dioxide and make oxygen for animals to use. The circular process is called the *oxygen-carbon dioxide cycle*. A cycle is a process that repeats itself over and over again.

From a pond or stream get a plant that

How can you show that plants manufacture oxygen?

lives under water. The plants that are put into aquariums can also be used. Put the plant into a large jar or an aquarium full of water. Place the jar in a sunny window. Place a large glass funnel upside down over the plant. Fill a test tube with water. Keep your finger over the end of the test tube so that you do not lose any water from it, and then place the test tube upside down over the part of the funnel that is uppermost in the jar.

After two or three days of sunlight, you will see gas in the upper part of the test tube. You may also see gas bubbles sticking to the upper surfaces of the leaves of the plant. This gas is oxygen.

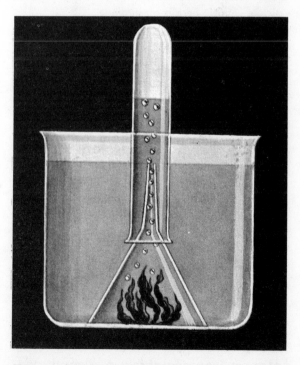

This experiment proves that plants give off oxygen.

The agricultural chemist plays an important role in the development of new fertilizers and insecticides. Shown here is an airplane "dusting" cultivated land with insecticide.

Most chemists specialize in not more than one or two fields. Thousands are employed in the pharmaceutical industry, developing new drugs and cosmetics for a world market.

The Branches of Chemistry

Chemistry is divided into several branches. Let us now explore some of them.

Man has been using chemistry in farming for a long

What is agricultural and food chemistry?

time without knowing it. As far back as the Middle Ages, farmers used to leave one field out of three idle each year. They did not know the scientific reason why this was a good idea,

but they did know that after a field had lain idle for a year, it grew better crops. Modern *agricultural chemists* know that growing plants remove certain compounds from the soil. During the year that a field is left idle, the soil gets back from the air and from ground water the compounds that the plants removed. The next year, plants will then be able to obtain from this field the compounds they need. Thanks to agricultural chemists, we know what com-

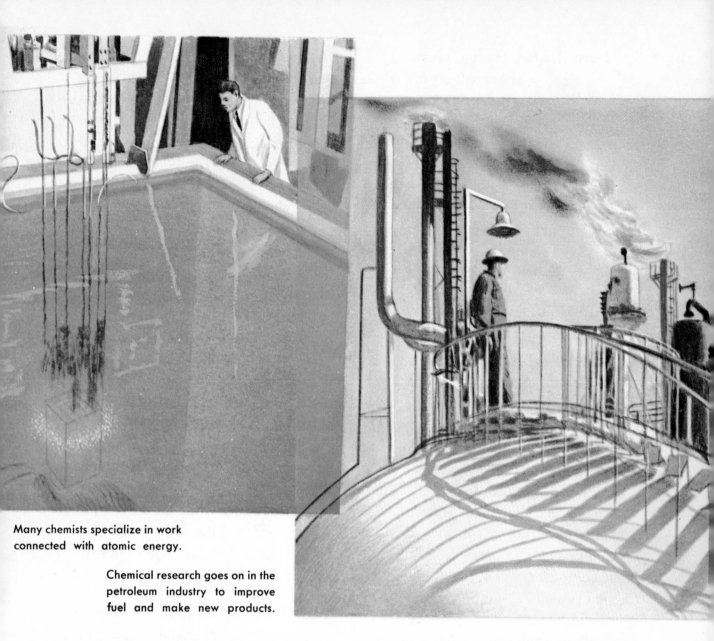

Many chemists specialize in work connected with atomic energy.

Chemical research goes on in the petroleum industry to improve fuel and make new products.

pounds plants need, and we put these compounds in the soil in the form of fertilizers. We no longer need to leave a field idle for a year.

Insects destroy millions of tons of food crops each year. This is a serious loss, but the amount of food insects would destroy if man did not fight them would be disastrous, probably causing starvation. It is the agricultural chemists who discover the sprays farmers must use to kill insects.

Once upon a time, well-fed cows in one part of the country were thin and sickly, while well-fed cows in other parts were fat and healthy. *Food chemists* learned that the healthy cows were fed corn that had the husks on the corn ears, but the sickly cows were fed wheat that had lost the wheat leaves during threshing. The husks are the leaves of the corn, and they have certain compounds cows need for health. When the sickly cows were fed green leaves, they too became healthy.

Food chemists are working on the possibility of making food for man from seaweed. As the population of the world increases, we soon may turn to the seas for other kinds of food besides fish.

We learned what organic chemistry is — the chemistry of carbon compounds. *Inorganic chemistry* includes the chemistry of all the other elements. One interesting group of compounds that modern inorganic chemists are working on is called *silicones*. The main element in these compounds is *silicon,* the second most abundant element in the earth's crust. Silicon, like carbon, can make compounds in the form of long chains. There are silicones that are rubbery and which won't crack in sub-zero weather. Other silicones are lubricants that will run in sub-zero weather. From these silicones are made gaskets, shock absorbers and other parts of machines that are used in polar regions. Do you have a coat that is "rainproof"? It is treated with a silicone that sheds water.

What is inorganic chemistry?

Transistors are electronic devices that make possible portable radios and giant computors. Transistors are made of the elements zirconium, germanium or selenium. Before inorganic chemists purified these elements, making efficient transistors was not possible.

We have learned that the slow burning of food materials in the tissues of the human body is a kind of chemical change. This is not the only

What is biochemistry?

chemical change that goes on in the body. On the contrary, in every part of the body chemical changes are constantly taking place. One group of chemists, the *biochemists,* have studied the chemistry of the body. They have found so many hundreds of complicated chemical changes in the human body that they are still at the beginning of their study. However, they already have knowledge gained from thousands of experiments, and this knowledge is enough to have revealed many wonderful things about the body.

Biochemists have learned how the chemicals of the blood react with the oxygen of the air to form the scab that stops you from bleeding to death from even a little cut.

Biochemists have learned that the digestion of food, the changing of digested food into body tissue, the use of stored food and the getting rid of waste products are all activities of the body that involve chemical changes.

Medical chemistry is really a branch of biochemistry, but medical chemistry concerns itself with the diseases of the body. Did you ever hear of anyone being told by his doctor to take a laboratory test of his blood or urine? The blood is the transportation division of the body. Chemi-

What is medical chemistry?

CHEMISTRY AS A HOBBY

CHEMISTRY IN COOKING

CHEMISTRY IN RESEARCH

cal compounds dissolved in the blood are constantly being carried from one part of the body to another. The urine carries some of the body's waste compounds. Medical chemists have learned pretty well what compounds should be carried in the blood and urine of a healthy person. If medical chemists make tests on the blood and urine and find too much or too little of certain compounds, or if they find new compounds in these two body liquids, they can tell a doctor which of the organs of the body are not working properly.

In our bodies are certain organs called *glands*. These glands make chemical compounds that are put into the body's blood stream. For instance, one of these glands is the *adrenal gland*. It makes a compound called *adrenalin*. This compound makes our hearts beat faster when we are frightened or angry or excited. If you were to inject some adrenalin into a rabbit, you could make the rabbit so ferocious that it would attack and fight a dog. Medical biochemists discovered adrenalin and the compounds made by our glands.

Every day, doctors lean heavily on the work of medical chemists. In many cases, diagnoses which were almost impossible a few years ago are now quick and sure, thanks to the knowledge of the chemical processes of the body painstakingly gathered by medical chemists.

Although chemistry had its beginning thousands of years ago in the work of the first alchemists, chemistry is really a young science. Consider simply the fact that organic chemists have discovered more than 300,000 carbon compounds. Does this mean that most carbon compounds have been discovered and that it is becoming harder and harder to discover a new compound? No, it is quite the contrary. Since "discovering" new chemical compounds actually means making them by combining already-known compounds in new ways, the more compounds that are discovered, the more material there is to work with to make new compounds. It is for this reason that almost every day some new chemical discovery is announced. It may be a new man-made fiber with properties that neither cotton, wool, flax nor silk can match. It may be a new drug that will cure one of the diseases that are now considered to be incurable.

In agriculture there is a continuing need for chemists to find new ways of fighting the diseases and insects that destroy so much of our food crops. As

Is there still a need for new chemists today?

There is still a great need today for chemists in Federal Government work, in private industry and in schools. Whether you enjoy chemistry as a professional pursuit or as a hobby, it is a fascinating subject to follow.

planetary space. If it had not been for chemists who developed powerful rocket fuels, the first artificial satellite could not have been launched. Still more powerful rocket fuels are needed, and so are new compounds that will help rockets to better resist the great heat caused by their re-entry into the earth's atmosphere.

There is, too, a great need for teachers of chemistry — in public schools and colleges — who are not only able to teach their students how to combine atoms and molecules into new compounds according to the laws of chemistry, but who are also able to inspire their students to use science for the good of mankind. Endless opportunities await the chemist to help make the world a more comfortable and more humane place in which to live. This is the noble purpose of chemistry.

the population of the world increases so rapidly, chemists are wondering whether it might not be possible for man to make and use chlorophyll to produce food directly from the very abundant raw materials, water and carbon dioxide. This would do away with the need to grow crops, only part of which are used for food.

Man has just begun to explore inter-

THE HOW AND WHY WONDER BOOK OF
The HUMAN BODY

Written by MARTIN KEEN
Illustrated by DARRELL SWEET
Editorial Production: DONALD D. WOLF

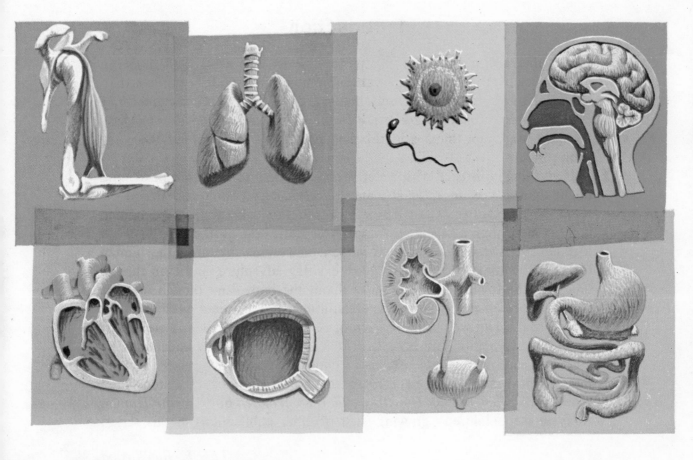

Edited under the supervision of
   Dr. Paul E. Blackwood
   Washington, D. C.

Text and illustrations approved by
   Oakes A. White, Brooklyn Children's Museum, Brooklyn, New York

GROSSET & DUNLAP • **Publishers** • **NEW YORK**

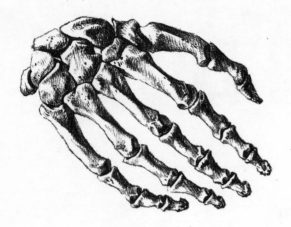

Introduction

It is the habit of scientists to explore, describe and explain all things in the universe. Little wonder, then, that the human body has been a constant object of study, for it is not only important but very close to home! *The How and Why Wonder Book of the Human Body* tells in a systematic way the most important things scientists and physicians have learned about the subject.

If you simply listened with a stethoscope to the beating of the heart, you might think it was an automatic machine. But if you could tune in on the remarkable activities of the brain cells, you would know that the human body is more than a machine. And as you learn how all the systems work together, you become amazed at what a marvelous organism the human body is. This makes the study of it an exciting adventure, and even though much has been known for centuries about the body, and though more is being discovered every year, there are still many unanswered questions.

The health and well-being of each of us depends on how well we understand our own bodies. This book is written to help us gain that understanding and may encourage many persons to choose a career of service in maintaining the health of others, perhaps as a nurse or doctor. Parents and schools will want to add *The How and Why Wonder Book of the Human Body* to their children's growing shelf of other publications in this series.

Paul E. Blackwood

Dr. Blackwood is a professional employee in the U. S. Office of Education. This book was edited by him in his private capacity and no official support or endorsement by the Office of Education is intended or should be inferred.

Library of Congress Catalog Card Number: 61-16034

Contents

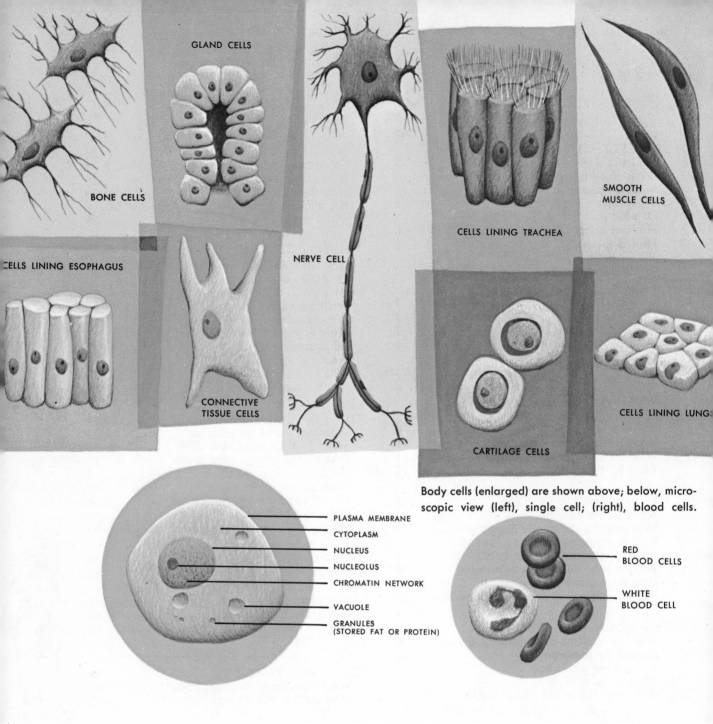

BONE CELLS

GLAND CELLS

CELLS LINING ESOPHAGUS

CONNECTIVE TISSUE CELLS

NERVE CELL

CELLS LINING TRACHEA

SMOOTH MUSCLE CELLS

CARTILAGE CELLS

CELLS LINING LUNGS

PLASMA MEMBRANE
CYTOPLASM
NUCLEUS
NUCLEOLUS
CHROMATIN NETWORK
VACUOLE
GRANULES
(STORED FAT OR PROTEIN)

RED BLOOD CELLS

WHITE BLOOD CELL

Body cells (enlarged) are shown above; below, microscopic view (left), single cell; (right), blood cells.

The Cell, the Body's Building Material

What do all living things have in common?

Perhaps at some time you have visited a zoo. There you saw huge elephants, tall giraffes, comical little monkeys, strange birds and many other kinds of animals. The animals in the different cages were so different that you must surely believe that they can have little in common.

Yet, all living things actually do have something in common. All living things are made of tiny units, called *cells*. The huge elephant is made of hundreds of billions of cells, and there are little animals whose whole body is but a single cell. The human body, too, is made of cells — billions of them.

Most cells are so small that you need a powerful magnifying lens to see one. Some cells are so small that you could put 250 thousand of them on the period at the end of this sentence. Others, however, are large enough to be seen with the unaided eye. Among these large cells are the root-hairs of plants, certain seaweeds, and the eggs of animals.

What do cells look like?

Cells are of many shapes. Some are round. Others look like bricks with rounded corners. Still others are long and hairlike. Some cells are shaped like plates, cylinders, ribbons or spiral rods.

What are the parts of a cell?

Looking through a microscope at a single cell from a human body, you can see that the cell is surrounded by membrane. This is the *cell membrane*. It surrounds the cell in the same way that a balloon surrounds the air within itself.

Within the cell membrane is a material that has a grainy appearance. This material is *cytoplasm,* which flows about within the cell membrane. Cytoplasm distributes nourishment within the cell and gets rid of the cell's waste products.

Within the cytoplasm is a large dot. This dot is really a sphere and is the cell's *nucleus*. The nucleus is the most important part of the cell. It directs the cell's living activities. The way in which the cell uses nourishment and oxygen, the way the cytoplasm gets rid of wastes, the way the cell reproduces — all these functions are regulated by the nucleus. If the nucleus is removed, the cell dies.

Of what material are cells made?

The cell membrane, the cytoplasm, and the nucleus of all cells are made of a material called *protoplasm*. Protoplasm is a living material and makes a living cell "alive." Scientists have analyzed protoplasm into the elements of which it is made. They have found protoplasm to

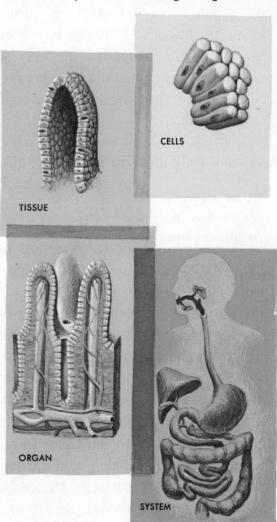

CELLS

TISSUE

ORGAN

SYSTEM

Tiny units are cells; a group of cells is a tissue; tissues form an organ; organs become unified system.

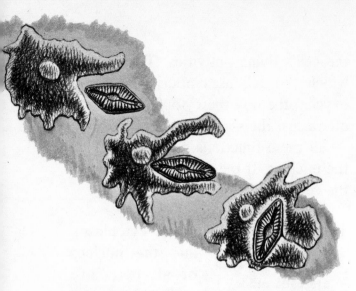

The amoeba is a microscopic mass of protoplasm. It is shown surrounding an organism on which it feeds.

be made of water and many other chemical substances. Although scientists know what these substances are and how much of each there is in protoplasm, no scientist thus far has been able to put them together properly so as to make living protoplasm. This fact tells us that protoplasm is a very complex material.

How are cells organized in a human body?

Cells not only differ in shape, but also in the work each kind of cell performs within a body. A group of cells, all of the same kind, that performs a particular kind of work, is called a *tissue*. For example, groups of cells that transmit impulses back and forth from the brain to other parts of the body make up nerve tissue. Other kinds of tissue are muscle tissue, connecting tissue, supporting tissue, and epithelial tissue. Epithelial tissue forms the outer layer of the skin, and the surface layer of the cavities in the body, such as the nose, throat, gullet and the stomach.

When different kinds of tissue are organized to perform a particular kind of work within a body, the tissues form an *organ*. An eye is an organ that performs the function of seeing. There are many parts to an eye and each part is made of a particular kind of tissue. When all the tissues of the eye work together while each tissue performs its separate task, then the eye can perform its function of seeing. Other examples of organs are the heart, liver, tongue and lungs.

Organs of the body are organized into unified *systems*. Each system performs a particular task for the body. For example, the digestive system, which includes the mouth, teeth, tongue, gullet, stomach, intestines and many glands, performs the function of digesting food.

How is the body like a machine?

Perhaps you have heard an automobile repairman say that a car's ignition system needed fixing. Or maybe it was the cooling system or the brake system. Each one of these systems is made up of several parts, and each system performs a particular task in running the car. All systems must work together if the car is to operate. Do you see the similarity between the automobile's systems and the organ systems of a human body?

The human body is a very wonderful machine. It is more complex, better made and can do more kinds of work under more conditions than any machine that man has so far constructed throughout his history.

Man has built giant electronic calculators that can solve mathematical problems in a fraction of the time that a human brain can. Calculating, however, is the only work the giant machine can do. It cannot decide what problems it should work on, nor when it should work on them, as the slower but more versatile human brain can. The great calculating machine, with its limited capacity, is so big that it takes up all the space around the walls of a large room, but the human brain, with its unlimited capacity, is smaller.

Why is the body more useful than a machine?

The calculating machine has thousands of parts, but the number of its parts does not even begin to equal the hundreds of millions of unit cells of which the human body is constructed. If the calculating machine breaks down, it must wait for a repairman to fix it. A break or a cut in some part of the human body can usually be repaired by the body itself.

Let us see in detail how this wonderful machine, the human body, works.

The Skin

When you look at a human body, the first thing you see is the *skin*. The average adult human body is covered with about eighteen square feet of skin. The skin varies in thickness. It is very thin over the eyelids, and quite thick on the palms of the hands and the soles of the feet.

How much skin is on a human body?

The skin is composed of two layers. The upper layer is the *epidermis*. This layer is made of dead, flattened cells, which are continually wearing off as we move around.

What are the parts of the skin?

This is a cutaway view of a single hair (right) showing the follicle, which is the opening, or depression, from which the hair grows.

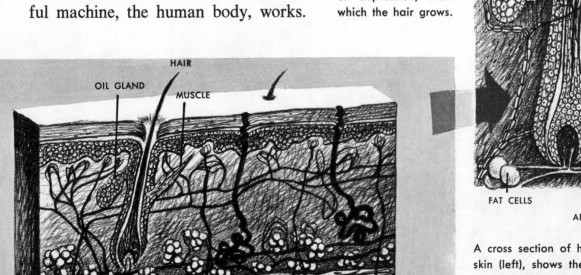

A cross section of human skin (left), shows the epidermis (top layer) and the dermis. The skin represents one of the largest organs of the entire human body.

HAIR

FAT CELLS VEIN ARTERY

HAIR
OIL GLAND
MUSCLE
FAT CELLS UNDERLYING MUSCLE
NERVE ENDINGS

The bottom of the epidermis is made of live cells that die and replace those that wear off on the surface.

Beneath the epidermis is the *dermis*. This layer of skin is made entirely of living cells. There are many small blood vessels and nerve endings in the dermis. Small coiled tubes in this layer open into the epidermis. These tubes are *sweat glands* and their openings are called *pores*. Hairs grow out of the skin and have their roots in the dermis. The openings from which hairs grow are called *hair follicles*.

The skin provides the body with a covering that is airtight, waterproof and, when unbroken, a bar to harmful bacteria.

What does the skin do?

The pigment, or coloring matter, of the skin screens out certain harmful rays of the sun.

The skin helps to regulate the temperature of the body. When the body surface is cold, the blood vessels in the skin contract and force blood deeper into the body. This prevents the body

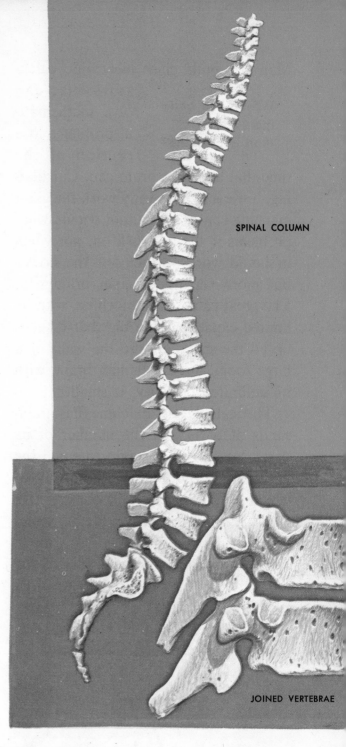

SPINAL COLUMN

JOINED VERTEBRAE

Cross section of human bone. Adults have 206 bones.

from losing much heat by radiation. When the body is too warm, the same blood vessels expand and bring more blood to the surface of the skin. This allows the body to lose heat by radiation. Also, the sweat glands pour out perspiration. The perspiration evaporates, and since evaporation is a cooling process, the skin is further cooled.

When perspiration flows out of the

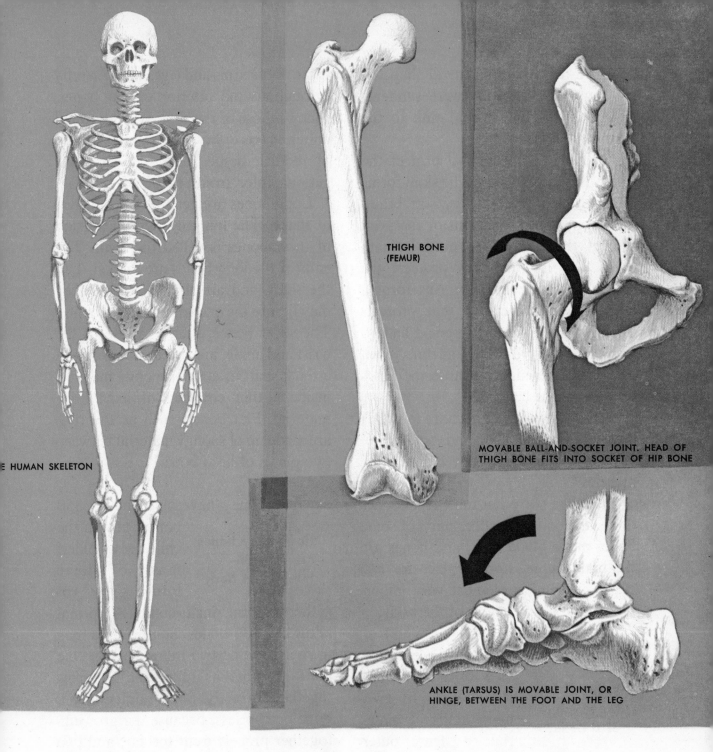

THIGH BONE
(FEMUR)

MOVABLE BALL-AND-SOCKET JOINT. HEAD OF
THIGH BONE FITS INTO SOCKET OF HIP BONE

E HUMAN SKELETON

ANKLE (TARSUS) IS MOVABLE JOINT, OR
HINGE, BETWEEN THE FOOT AND THE LEG

pores, it carries with it certain dissolved body wastes.

The skin is a sense organ because there are many nerve endings in the skin.

Although people do not ordinarily consider the skin to be an organ of the body, you can see by its structure and all the things it performs for the body that it really is an organ.

The Bones

What is the purpose of the skeleton? If you suddenly removed the poles from a circus tent, the tent would collapse. The poles support the soft, pliable canvas of the tent. They also help to give the tent its shape. The *bones* of the human skeleton support the softer parts of the body

9

and give the body its general shape. If the skeleton of a body were suddenly removed, the body would sink to the floor in a shapeless mass.

The bones also help to protect the softer parts of the body. The skull forms a strong case for the very soft brain. Two bony sockets in front of the skull protect the eyes. The spinal column forms a bony tube that protects the delicate spinal cord. The ribs form a hard elastic framework that protects the heart and lungs. If a person had no ribs and bumped into someone, even a small bump might collapse the lungs or damage the heart.

Bones also provide anchors to which muscles are attached, and bones provide leverage for the movement of the muscles.

There are two other things that bones do for the body: the inner parts of some bones make blood cells; and bones are the body's chief storage place for calcium, a chemical element very important to the sound health of the body.

You can see, by looking at a cutaway view of a bone, that

What is the structure of a bone? it consists of two main kinds of material: a dense outer material and a spongy, porous inner material. The hard outer material, that gives a bone its shape and strength, is made mostly of compounds of the chemical elements *calcium* and *phosphorus*. The soft inner part of the bone is called *marrow*. Most marrow is yellowish in color. It is made up of fat cells and is simply a storage depot for fat. Toward the ends of long bones, like

those of the arms and legs, and generally throughout the interior of flat bones, such as those of the skull and the spinal column, there are patches and streaks of reddish tissue. This reddish tissue gets its color from red blood cells.

Long bones are generally cylindrical in shape. The long, cylindrical portion of these bones is called the *shaft*. The ends of the long bones are thicker than the shaft, and are shaped so that they may fit into the ends of adjoining bones. The short bones, such as those of the wrist and ankle, are composed mostly of a thick shaft of elastic, spongy material inside a thin covering of hard bone material. Flat bones, such as the ribs, are made up of spongy material between two plates of hard bone.

An infant may have as many as 350 bones, but as the

How many bones are there in the human body? child grows older, many of these bones grow together to form single bones. A normal adult has 206 bones. Some adults may have a bone or two more, because the bones they had as infants did not grow together correctly. Some adults have a bone or two less, because the growing-together process went too far, and two bones of their ankles or wrists that should have remained separate may have grown together.

The skull is made up of twenty-nine bones. The round part of the skull, the part that encases the brain, is called the *cranium,* and consists of eight bones. The face, including the lower jaw, consists of fourteen bones. There are three tiny bones in each ear. And

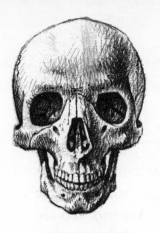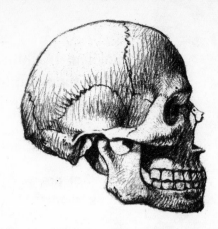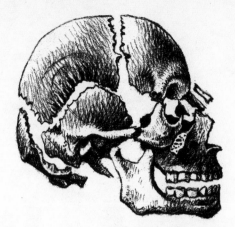

Front view of the human skull (left); side view (center); and side view with bones separated (right). The cranium, the part of the skull enclosing the brain, is composed of bones which are held together by immovable joints.

there is a single bone — the *hyoid bone* — in the throat.

The spinal column consists of twenty-six hollow cylinders of bone called *vertebrae*. If you strung together twenty-six spools of thread on a stiff wire in the shape of a very open letter S, you would have constructed something that looks much like the human spinal column.

The chest consists of twenty-five bones: one breast bone, called the *sternum*, and twenty-four ribs. Seven pairs of ribs attach to the spinal column at one end and the sternum at the other. Three pairs of ribs attach only to the spinal column, curve around to the front, but do not meet the sternum. And two pairs of ribs, called *floating ribs*, extend from the spine only part-way around to the front.

There are two collar bones, and two shoulder bones. Each arm consists of one upper-arm bone and two lower-arm bones. There are eight bones in the wrist. The palm of each hand is made up of five bones, and fourteen bones make up the fingers of a hand.

There are two hip bones. Each leg has one thigh bone, one kneecap, one shinbone, and one bone on the other side of the lower leg.

The ankle of each foot consists of seven bones and the foot, itself, of five, while fourteen bones make up the toes of each foot.

Every bone in the body — except one — meets with another bone. The one bone that does not meet another bone is the U-shaped hyoid bone in the throat.

How are the bones connected?

The meeting places of the bones are called *joints*. There are two kinds of joints: those about which the adjoining bones do not move, and those about which the bones do move freely. The bones of the cranium are held together by joints of the first kind. These are immovable joints.

Holding these bones together is a kind of very tough, springy tissue, called *cartilage*. Cartilage also joins together the bones of the spinal column. The springy nature of cartilage makes it a good shock absorber. If the lower parts of the spine receive a blow, the cartilage rings that join each vertebra to the one above it, absorb the shock, so that the brain does

What holds the bones together?

11

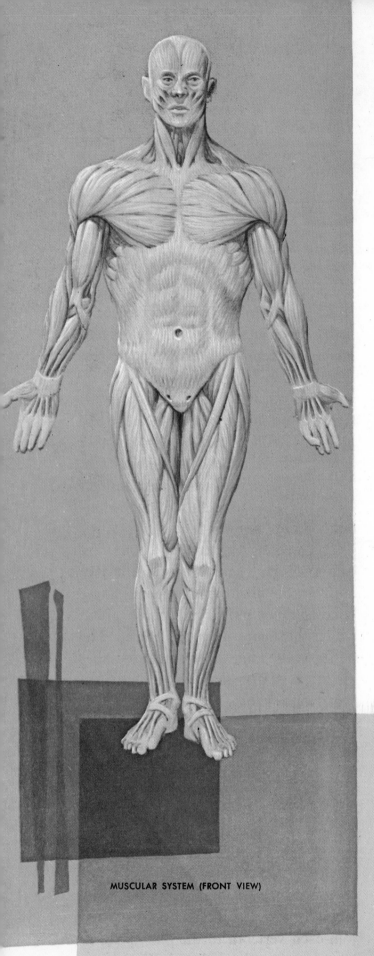

MUSCULAR SYSTEM (FRONT VIEW)

not feel the blow. If this were not so, every time you took a step, your brain would receive a jolt.

The bones at movable joints are held together by thick cords

What are ligaments?

of tough, stringy tissue called *ligaments*. To aid movement, at least one of the two adjoining bones has a small hollow that contains a lubricating fluid. This fluid helps the bones move smoothly over one another, just as oil helps the parts of an engine move over one another.

All the bones of the body and their connecting cartilage and ligaments make up the body's *skeletal system*.

The Muscular System

The bones of the human body have no

What are the muscles?

way of moving themselves. The muscles of the body move the bones and there are more than 600 muscles to move the parts of the skeleton. Muscles make up more than half the weight of the human body.

Muscles are made of bunches of

CROSS SECTION THROUGH MUSCLE

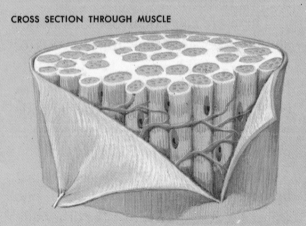

muscular tissue held tightly together. Muscular tissue is very fibrous, so that a muscle is somewhat like a bunch of rubber bands bound tightly together.

Beef is the muscle of steers. With a pin, pick apart a piece of roast beef. You will easily be able to separate it into long, thin strands that are fibers of muscle tissue. If you have a microscope, place a very thin muscle fiber under a cover-glass upon a glass slide. You will then be able to see that muscle tissue is made up of spindle-shaped cells.

How can you see muscle fibers?

A typical muscle is thick in the middle and tapers gradually toward the ends. It is the ends of a muscle that are attached to bones. One end of a muscle is anchored to a bone that the muscle cannot move. This attachment is called the *origin* of the muscle. The other end is attached to a bone that the muscle is intended to move. This attachment is called the *insertion* of the muscle. For example, the

How are muscles attached to bones?

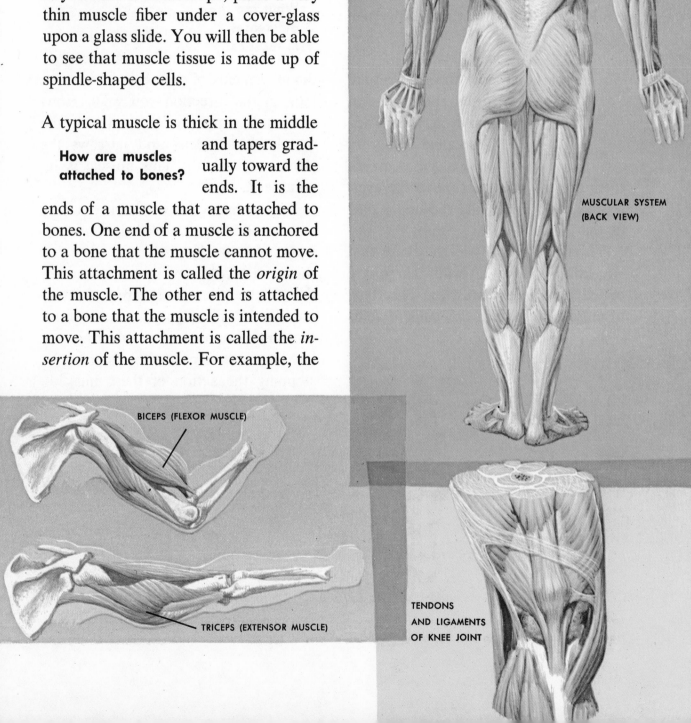

MUSCULAR SYSTEM (BACK VIEW)

BICEPS (FLEXOR MUSCLE)

TRICEPS (EXTENSOR MUSCLE)

TENDONS AND LIGAMENTS OF KNEE JOINT

muscle at the front of the upper arm — called the *biceps* — has its origin at the shoulder bone, and its insertion is just below the elbow joint on the bone that is on the thumb side of the forearm. The actual attachment of the end of a muscle to a bone is usually accomplished by a short, tough cord of much the same kind of tissue that makes up ligaments. This connective cord is called a *tendon*.

All the muscles of the body and their tendons make up the *muscular system* of the body.

The muscles that move the skeleton are

What are the two kinds of muscle?

ones that we can move at will. They are called *voluntary muscles*. Among them are the ones that move the eyes, tongue, soft palate and the upper part of the gullet.

There are muscles in the body that we cannot move at will. These are called *involuntary muscles*. This type of muscle is found in the walls of veins and arteries, stomach, intestines, gall bladder, the lower parts of the gullet and in several other internal organs. Thousands of tiny involuntary muscles in the skin move the hair. When you are chilled or frightened and have goose flesh, or goose pimples, the little lumps on your skin are due to the tiny muscles in the skin pulling your hairs erect.

The eye provides a good distinction be-

What are the differences in muscles?

tween voluntary and involuntary muscles. Voluntary muscles enable you to control the movements of your eye, in order to look in the direction you wish. However, you cannot control at will the muscle that widens and narrows the pupil of your eye. This muscle is involuntary.

But the distinction between voluntary and involuntary muscles does not always hold true. For instance, when you shiver with cold or fright, the muscles that shake your body are voluntary muscles. Ordinarily, you can control these muscles, but , when shivering, you have no control over either starting or stopping the action of these muscles.

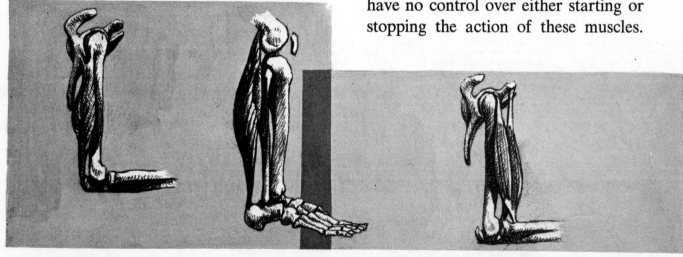

Lowering the arm (left) is an example of a first-class lever, as in a seesaw; rising on the toes (center), a second-class lever, as in a rowing oar; flexing, or "making a muscle" (right), a third-class lever, as in a fishing rod.

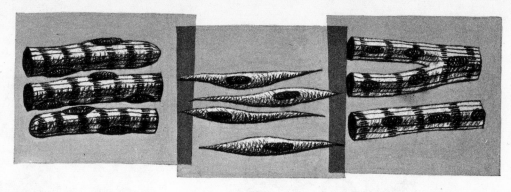

The stringlike matter making up voluntary muscles is known as fiber. Three kinds of muscle fiber are shown here (left to right): skeletal, smooth, cardiac.

They act as if they were involuntary. Certain circus performers can swallow various objects, and then, at will, bring them up without difficulty. These performers have learned to control their involuntary stomach and lower-gullet muscles, as though they were voluntary muscles.

How do muscles move? Muscle tissue is made of cells whose cytoplasm can contract. When the muscle contracts, it becomes short, and thereby pulls on the bone in which it is inserted. When you want to show someone how strong you are and you "make a muscle" by contracting your biceps, your forearm is pulled up toward your shoulder. If you want to lower your arm, you relax your biceps and contract your *triceps,* the muscle on the underside of the arm. The contraction of the triceps pulls the forearm straight. You can see that the two muscles of the upper arm work as a team or pair. All the voluntary muscles of the body work in pairs.

How do joints help muscles to move bones? One way to increase the power used to do work is to apply that power to a lever. A lever is a device that increases work power or range of motion. The joints in the human body act as levers that increase the power of a muscle or increase the distance through which the muscle can move a bone.

If you raise yourself on your toes, you are making use of one kind of lever. The muscles that form the calves of your legs have to do the work of lifting your whole body. You would need to have much larger calf muscles if they had to undergo the strain of lifting your body by a direct pull. Yet you easily raise yourself on your toes, because your foot acts as a lever.

In the act of raising yourself on your toes, your weight bears straight down on the point where your shinbone rests on your ankle bone. The muscles of your calf pull upward on your heel bone, and your foot pivots upward on the fulcrum — the point around which the lever moves — which is formed by the bones that make up the ball of your foot. (Although we say that we raise ourselves on our toes, we actually raise ourselves on the balls of our feet and steady ourselves with our toes.)

If you reach down and grasp the back of your foot just above your heel, you can feel the strong tendon — called the *Achilles tendon* — that connects the muscles of your calf to your heel bone. If, now, you raise yourself on the ball of your foot, you can feel the calf muscles tighten and bulge as they contract and pull upward on your heel.

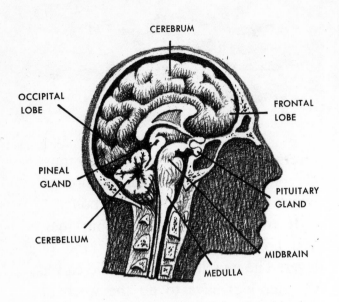

Cutaway view of the skull showing location of brain.

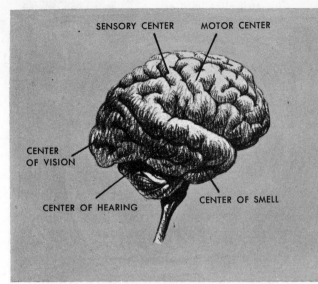

Parts of the brain control several of our activities.

The Brain and Nerves

Suppose you have dropped your pencil on the floor and want to pick it up. This is a very easy thing to do, something you can accomplish with hardly any thought or difficulty. Yet this simple action causes you to use dozens of your voluntary muscles.

What controls the movements of the body?

First, you have to locate the pencil. This requires you to move your eyes, and probably also to turn your head, until you have brought the pencil into view. Then you must bend down to reach the pencil, grasp it, and then straighten up again. Not only do dozens of voluntary muscles bring about your motions, but they must do so in just the right order. It would be futile to attempt to grasp the pencil before you bent down to bring your hand within reach. Clearly something is controlling the motions of your muscles. What is it?

The movements of your muscles are controlled by your brain which works through a system of nerves distributed throughout your body. The brain and the nerves, together, make up the body's *nervous system*.

The brain occupies the upper half of the skull. The largest part of the brain, called the *cerebrum*, consists of two deeply-wrinkled hemispheres of nerve tissue, one hemisphere on each side of the head.

What is the cerebrum?

All of man's conscious activities are controlled by his cerebrum. It enables him to remember, perceive things, solve problems and understand meanings — in short, to think. Thanks to man's most highly-developed cerebrum, he is the most intelligent of all animals.

At the back of the skull, and almost covered by the cerebrum, is the *cerebellum*. This part of the brain, too, consists of two hemispheres.

What is the cerebellum?

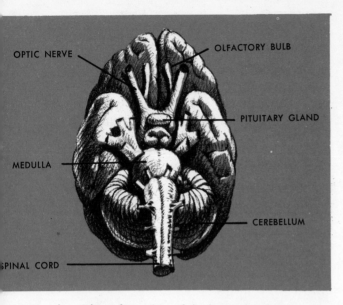

OPTIC NERVE
OLFACTORY BULB
PITUITARY GLAND
MEDULLA
CEREBELLUM
SPINAL CORD

An undersurface view of the brain showing its parts.

The cerebellum coordinates muscular activity. It is the cerebellum that is responsible for man's ability to learn habits and develop skills. As an infant you learned, after many tries and falls, to stand upright. Learning to walk was another accomplishment that took much time and effort. Now, standing and walking are habits to which you need give no thought, yet both these activities require the use of many muscles in exactly the right order. The cerebellum automatically controls these muscles.

Have you learned to skate or ride a bicycle? At first, you had to think about each move you made, but soon the movements became automatic, so that you did not have to think unless an unusual situation arose. When you were learning, your cerebrum was in control of your movements as you thought about just which muscles you were going to use next. Later, when you knew how to make each movement correctly, your cerebellum took over con-

The brain and spinal cord make up the central nervous system. The nerves which branch out of this nervous system form the peripheral nervous system.

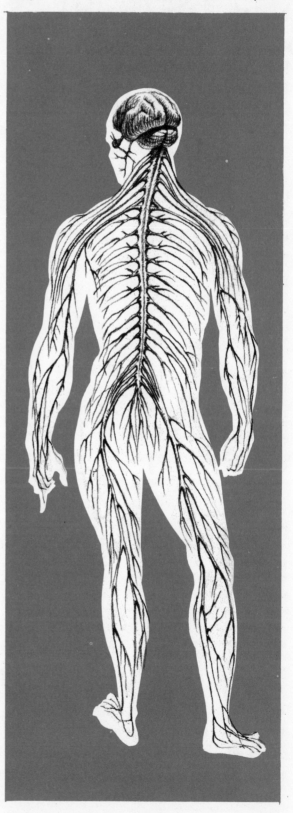

17

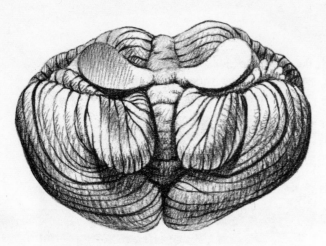

The cerebellum coordinates man's mind and muscles.

trol from your cerebrum. Although the cerebellum's muscular control is automatic, it is important to remember that the muscles it controls are voluntary muscles.

The involuntary muscles are controlled **What is the medulla?** by a small part of the brain that is at the top of the spinal cord. This is the *medulla*. It is a little more than an inch long and is really a thickening

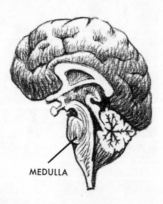

The medulla is a bulblike enlargement of the spinal cord. It carries and sends out nerve impulses which control circulation of blood, breathing, digestion and other processes, too.

MEDULLA

of the spinal cord. The medulla controls the beating of the heart, the rate of breathing, the movements of the stomach and intestines, the movements of the gullet when swallowing and other vital activities of the body.

The *spinal cord* extends downward from **What does the spinal cord look like?** the medulla through the protecting bony rings of the spinal column. The cord is cylindrical in shape, with an outer covering of supporting cells and blood vessels, and an inner, H-shaped core of nerve fibers. The spinal cord extends through four-fifths the length of the spine, and is a little longer in men than in women, averaging sixteen and one-half inches in length. It weighs just about one ounce.

Twelve pairs of nerves branch off the spinal cord and pass through the base of the skull into the brain. Thirty-one other pairs branch off the spinal cord throughout its length. These nerve branches run to all the organs of the body, where they branch again and again, until the smallest branches are nerves which are so thin that they cannot be seen with the unaided eye.

Nerves that extend upward from the spinal cord to the brain pass through the medulla where they cross. Thus, the left side of the brain controls the right side of the body, while the right side of the brain controls the left side of the body.

An army division is composed of many **How is the nervous system like an army telephone network?** thousands of men who perform a wide variety of duties. In order to control the activities of so many soldiers, it is necessary to have some system by which the commanding general can learn what is going on in all the units of his division and thus, to give orders to any of these units. In order to accomplish this, a telephone network is set up.

When a battle is in progress, soldiers posted near the battle line can telephone reports of action back to their headquarters in order to inform the general of the situation. The general gets the messages from these posts. Using this information, and calling on his training and experience, he issues orders to be followed by soldiers under his command. These orders travel back along the same telephone wires.

Let us follow a similar situation within the human body. Let us suppose that you have accidently knocked a pencil off your desk and want to pick it up. When the sound of the falling pencil reaches your ears, it causes elec-

trical impulses to move from your ears along two nerves — auditory nerves — and then to your brain. Your ears are similar to the posts near the battle line, your nerves similar to the telephone wires, and the electrical impulses similar to the messages that move along the wires.

When the brain receives electrical impulses from the ears, a particular part of the cerebrum perceives the impulses as sound, and passes this information on to another part of the cerebrum, one that is concerned with recognition. This part of the brain calls on the part that stores information —

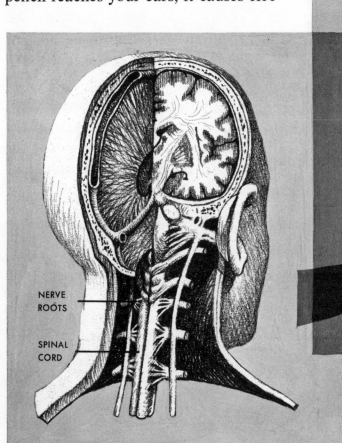

NERVE
ROOTS

SPINAL
CORD

(Left): Cutaway view of back of the head. (Above): Part of the backbone, also known as the spine, spinal column and vertebral column. It consists of bones called vertebrae which surround the spinal cord.

the memory. If you have ever before heard a pencil fall, your memory recognizes the sound. Now, you are aware of what has happened.

This situation is similar to that of the general who gets battle reports, and then calls on his training and past experience to help him get a clear picture of what is taking place at the battle-front.

Once your brain is aware of the fallen pencil, it decides to pick up the pencil. Electrical impulses go from your brain to the muscles of your eyes, which then move about seeking to bring the pencil into view. This is similar to that of the general who sends messages to front-line posts asking for more information on the battle.

When the pencil is brought into view, electrical impulses flash back to your cerebrum, which must again go through the processes of perception and recognition, in order to identify the pencil. Here we have new reports coming back to the commanding general who interprets them.

Having located the pencil, your cerebrum now sends hundreds of electrical impulses along nerves to the many muscles that must be moved when you bend over, reach out your arm, close your fingers around the pencil, and then straighten up again. These impulses and the responding muscular movements are similar to messages from the general going out over the telephone wires and the soldiers acting upon the general's orders.

Nerve cells, also called *neurons,* are

What are nerve cells?

specially constructed so as to carry nerve impulses from one part of the body to another. Nerve tissue can conduct extremely small amounts of electricity. Nerve impulses are actually small amounts of electricity.

Each neuron has a central portion, or

What are the parts of a neuron?

cell body, that has a nucleus, cytoplasm and a cell membrane. From one side of the cell body there extend very slender branching threads of protoplasm.

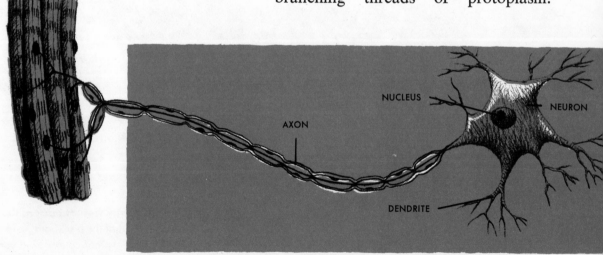

NUCLEUS

NEURON

AXON

DENDRITE

Nerve impulses from a neuron travel to the nerve endings of a muscle (left).

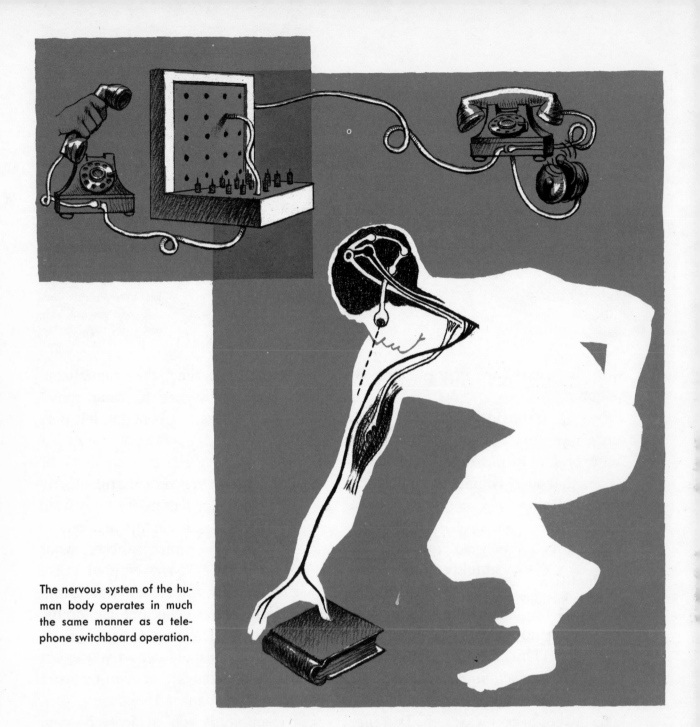

The nervous system of the human body operates in much the same manner as a telephone switchboard operation.

These tiny nerve fibers are called *dendrites*. They look much like twigs at the end of a tree branch. From the other side of the cell body there extends a fairly thick nerve fiber — surrounded by a fatty sheath — which ends in slender, branching threads of protoplasm. These nerve fibers are called *axons*. Some axons are very short, while others are as much as three feet long. Dendrites conduct nerve impulses to the cell body. Axons carry impulses away from the cell body.

Nerve tissue is made up of a series of neurons arranged so that the branching threads of protoplasm of an axon intermingle with the dendrites of the neighboring neuron. However, the two sets of branches do not actually touch. The gap between the branches is called a *synapse*. When an impulse moves along a nerve, it must jump across the syn-

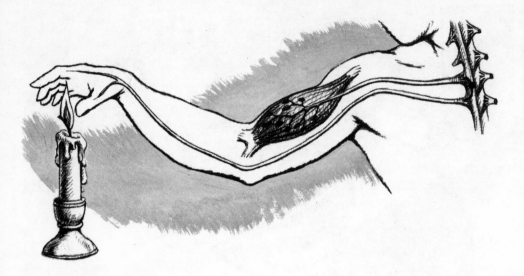

A simple reflex action takes place when you touch a candle flame. The arm muscles contract and you pull your arm away very quickly.

apse between one neuron and its neighbor.

Nerves are divided into two kinds: *sensory nerves* that carry impulses from sense organs to the brain, and *motor nerves* that carry command impulses to the muscles.

If you touch a very hot radiator, you

What is a reflex action?

quickly jerk your hand away. You do not think about pulling your hand away — you act automatically. This automatic action is called a *reflex action*.

In a reflex action, the nerve impulse takes a special pathway, called a *reflex arc*. In the case of your touching the hot radiator, the impulse moved from the skin where it came in contact with the radiator along a sensory nerve to your spinal cord. Here the impulse set off another impulse in a motor nerve running from your spinal cord to your arm muscles. The muscles contracted and pulled your hand away from the radiator. This action took place in about one-tenth of a second.

At the same time, the original sensory impulse traveled up your spinal cord to your brain, where you felt it as pain.

Reflex actions are very useful in pro-

How are reflex actions helpful?

tecting the body from harm. If you had to think about what movements to make

when suddenly threatened with harm, you might become confused and do the wrong thing. The automatic action of your reflexes usually causes you to act correctly and quickly enough to avoid or lessen the danger threatening you. For example, if you suddenly become aware of an object flying through the air toward your face, reflex actions cause you to dodge the object and to close your eyes tightly.

Sit comfortably in a chair, and cross

How can you demonstrate a reflex action?

your right leg over the upper part of your left leg. Feel around just below the

kneecap of your right leg for a tendon

that runs downward from the kneecap. With the edge of the fingers of your right hand strike this tendon sharply — though not too hard, of course. If you do this correctly, the lower part of your right leg will jump upward, bending from the knee joint. After you have learned to cause this reflex action, wait a few minutes and try it again. This time, you may note that your leg is already in motion before you feel your fingers strike the knee.

The Senses

We are made aware of the world around us by means of our *senses*. For many centuries, man believed that human beings had only five senses: *sight, hearing, touch, smell,* and *taste.* Modern scientists have added to the list the senses of *pressure, heat, cold* and *pain*.

What are the senses?

There are several steps in the process of sensing. A stimulus acts on the nerves in one of the sense organs. Nerve impulses from the sense organ travel to the brain. In the brain, the impulses are interpreted as a feeling or sensation. For instance, if you stick your finger with a needle, nerve endings in the skin of your finger are stimulated to send impulses to your brain, which interprets the impulses as pain.

It is important to note that, although the brain interprets the impulses as pain, the pain is not felt in the brain, but rather in the finger; that is, the sense organ.

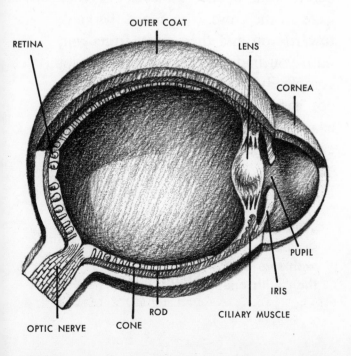

CROSS SECTION OF THE HUMAN EYE

RETINA

OUTER COAT

LENS

CORNEA

PUPIL

IRIS

CILIARY MUSCLE

ROD

CONE

OPTIC NERVE

The organs of sight are the *eyes*. A human eye is shaped like a ball and is about an inch in diameter. The eye is surrounded by a tough white protective covering. At the front of the eye, there is a transparent circular portion in this covering. Just behind this transparent portion is a space filled with a clear liquid. At the back of this space is a circular tissue with a hole in it. The tissue is called the *iris,* and the hole is the *pupil*. The iris is the colored part of the eye. On the

What does the eye look like?

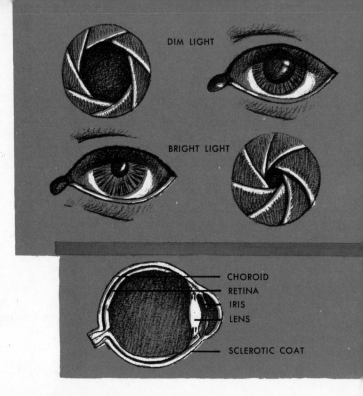

DIM LIGHT

BRIGHT LIGHT

CHOROID
RETINA
IRIS
LENS

SCLEROTIC COAT

inner edge of the iris, around the pupil, is a ring of tiny muscles sensitive to light. In bright light, these muscles contract and narrow the pupil. In dim light, the muscles relax and widen the pupil.

If you stand in front of a mirror in a brightly-lit room, you can easily see the pupil of your eye widen and narrow. Cover one eye with your hand for about a minute and a half. Suddenly remove your hand, and look at the eye that was covered. You will see the pupil narrow.

Behind the iris is a transparent circular lens made of tough tissue. **How do we see?** Muscles attached to the rim of this lens can focus it upon near or far objects. A beam of light passing through the lens is turned upside down and is reversed from right to left. After passing through the lens, light traverses a large spherical cavity that makes up the bulk of the eye. This cavity is filled with a clear liquid through which light passes easily. Around the inner surface of this cavity is a coating of special nerve endings that are sensitive to light. This sensitive coating is the *retina*. The nerve endings connect with the *optic nerve* that leads to the brain.

Light, reflected from an object and entering the eye, is focused by the lens as a reversed image on the retina. The nerve impulses arriving at the brain from the retina are interpreted as an image of the object.

This interpretation also reverses the directions of the image as it was projected on the retina, so that we do not see things upside down and backward.

At the point where the optic nerve enters the eye, there is **What is the blind spot?** no retina, and consequently, this area is not light-sensitive. This point, which is just below the center of the back of the eye, is called the *blind spot*.

You can prove the existence of this blind spot in the following manner. Note the cross and the dot on this page. Close your left eye, and hold this page before your open right eye. Fix your gaze on the cross. Now move the book toward you and then away from you, until you find the point where the dot completely disappears. At this point the dot is focused by the lens of the eye exactly on your blind spot. Hence, you can't see the dot.

✚ ●

Place a table directly beneath a light, **Why do we see better with two eyes than with one?** so that objects near the center of the table cast no shadows. Stand about eight feet in front of the

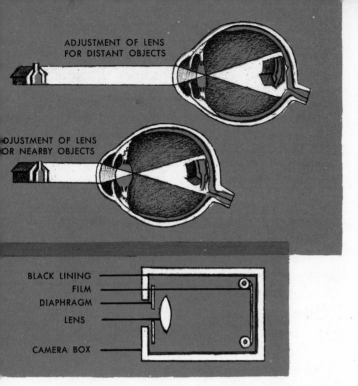

ADJUSTMENT OF LENS FOR DISTANT OBJECTS

ADJUSTMENT OF LENS FOR NEARBY OBJECTS

BLACK LINING
FILM
DIAPHRAGM
LENS
CAMERA BOX

The characteristics and operation of both the human eye and the camera eye show remarkable similarity.

table. Crouch down so that your eyes are on a level with the top of the table, and close one eye.

Ask someone to stand a thread-spool at the center of the table. Also ask him to place another spool of the same size about four inches in front or in back of the first spool, but not to tell you whether the second spool is before or behind the first. Try to guess the location of the second spool. Try this several times, keeping a record of your correct guesses. You will probably have a poor score.

With both eyes open, repeat your guessing. This time, you should have a nearly-perfect score. Why?

When we look at an object with both eyes, a slightly different image is projected on the retina of each eye. This is true because each eye sees the object from a slightly different angle. The result is that the brain's interpretation of the two images provides the viewer with a single, three-dimensional image of the object. The two images also pro-

vide the viewer with a perception of depth that enables him to make judgments of farness and nearness. This is why you had a better score when judging the locations of the spools with both eyes open.

The *ears* are the organs of hearing. The part of the ear on the outside of the head helps to a slight extent to direct sound waves into the ear. Sound waves entering the ear strike the eardrum, or *tympanic membrane,* and cause it to vibrate. This membrane stretches taughtly across the whole diameter of the ear passage. Touching the inner surface of the eardrum is a tiny bone called the *malleus* or hammer. The malleus connects by a joint to another little bone, the *incus* or anvil. And the incus is jointed to a third bone, the *stapes* or stirrup — so named because it looks like a stirrup. Below

What does the ear look like?

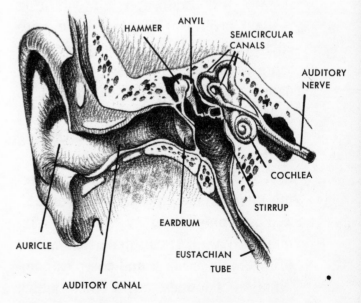

HAMMER ANVIL SEMICIRCULAR CANALS AUDITORY NERVE AUDITORY CANAL AURICLE EARDRUM EUSTACHIAN TUBE STIRRUP COCHLEA

A cross section of the human ear, showing its parts.

25

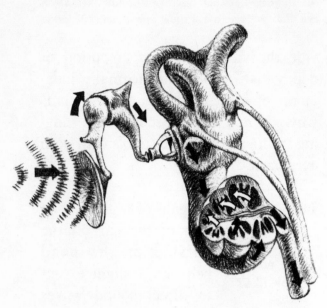

Arrows show path of sound through the inner ear.

presence of an orchestra. Also, your hearing organs can be activated by such small volumes of sound as those which come from a pencil moving over a sheet of paper on the other side of a room from the hearer.

Blindfold yourself with a handkerchief, and sit on a chair placed in the middle of a room. Ask someone to move quietly to any part of the room and clap his hands once. Point to where you think he is. Repeat this activity several times as your aide moves quietly from place to place about the room. Have your helper keep score of the number of times you have pointed correctly to the location at which he clapped his hands.

Why do we hear better with two ears than with one?

Place a hand tightly over one ear, and repeat the whole experiment. Repeat it a third time, covering the other ear.

If your sense of hearing is normal, you will find that your score of correct locations was poorer when you listened with only one ear. From this you can readily understand that using two ears gives you a better perception of sound direction, just as using two eyes gives you a better perception of visual depth.

and inward from the stirrup are three small cavities filled with liquid that are separated from each other by membranes. The innermost of these membranes connects with nerves that go to the brain.

When sound waves cause the eardrum to vibrate, the eardrum causes the malleus to vibrate, too. The vibrating malleus strikes against the incus with each vibration. The incus passes the vibration to the stirrup, which, in turn, causes the liquid in the cavities to vibrate. Vibration in the innermost cavity sets up impulses in the nerves that go to the cerebrum. That part of the cerebrum concerned with the sense of hearing interprets the impulses as sound.

How do we hear?

This complicated system works remarkably well. It can make you aware of a very wide range and complex combination of sounds, such as those which reach your ear when you are in the

The organ of smell is the *nose*. When taking a breath, you may draw into your nose certain gases intermingled with the gases of which air is made. When the added gases come into contact with a small patch of epithelial cells on the upper part of the

Why do we smell odors?

inner surface of your nose, the cells cause impulses to travel along a pair of nerves to your cerebrum, where the impulses are interpreted as odors.

Just how this process takes place is not clearly known. However, since the inside of the nose is always damp, scientists believe that the odorous gases dissolve in the dampness and cause a chemical reaction that stimulates nerve endings in the epithelial cells. This causes the cells to send impulses along the nerves.

Not all gases react with the organ of smell to set up sensations of odor. This is why we call only certain gases — those that do react — odors or smells. The more of an odorous gas that comes into contact with the organ of smell, the stronger is the sensation of odor. This is why we usually draw deep breaths when we sniff about to locate the source of an odor.

Can the sense of smell get "tired" or "lost"? The sense of smell seems to become fatigued easily; that is, the sensation of odor fades after a short time. Perhaps you have entered a room in which you found a strong odor. After a few minutes, however, you did not seem to notice the odor at all.

The discharge of mucus that accompanies a severe cold will cause you to lose your sense of smell, because the mucus forms a thick covering over the epithelial cells of the nose and prevents odorous gases from coming in contact with the cells.

The sense of smell is highly developed among a large part of the animal kingdom. These animals use smell as their chief means of learning about their surroundings. In human beings, however, the sense of smell is only mildly developed.

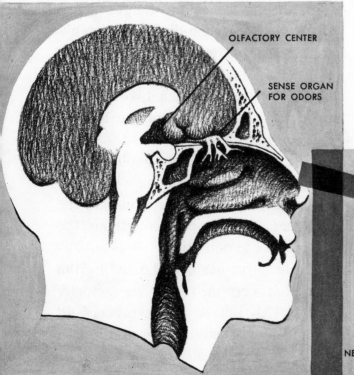

OLFACTORY CENTER

SENSE ORGAN FOR ODORS

The cutaway view of the head shows the sense organ for odors and the olfactory center. The cross section is an enlarged part of the lining of the nose.

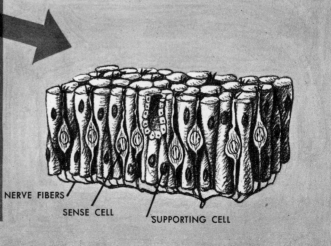

NERVE FIBERS

SENSE CELL

SUPPORTING CELL

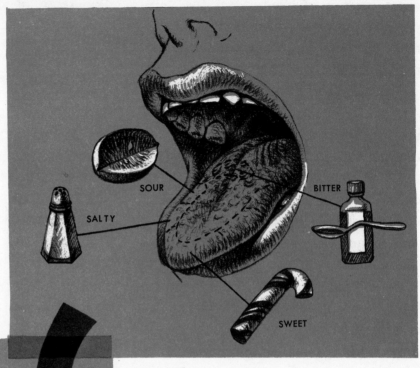

Different taste buds in the tongue are responsible for different taste sensations.

SOUR

SALTY

BITTER

SWEET

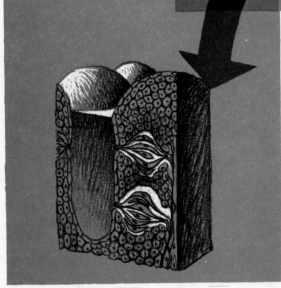

Taste buds are shown in this cross section of tongue.

Small organs, called *taste buds,* are lo-

How do we taste things?

cated just below the surface of the tongue and in three places in the throat. Certain materials taken into the mouth cause taste buds to produce the sensation of taste. Just how this sensation is brought about is not known. Taste, like smell, is probably the result of a mild chemical reaction. Taste sen-

sations may be divided into *sweet, salty, sour* and *bitter.*

Not all tastes are detected by the same taste buds. Those taste buds at the sides and tip of the tongue transmit impulses of saltiness to the brain. The buds at the tip of the tongue detect sweetness, those near the base detect bitterness and those on the sides detect sourness. Thus, there are certain areas of the tongue in which two kinds of taste buds are located: these are the sides and the tip.

The sense of taste is complicated by the fact that one taste may mask or counteract another. For example, the sweetness of sugar will counteract the sourness of lemon juice.

Taste is further complicated by the fact that certain tastes are actually odors. This is true of the taste of an onion. If a bad cold causes you to lose your sense of smell, you will not be able to taste an onion.

How do we feel things? The chief organs of feeling are free nerve endings in the epithelial cells of the body. On the outside of the body, the skin is the organ of feeling; within the body, it is the epithelial cells that line all cavities, such as the mouth, throat, stomach, intestines, ears, chest and sinuses.

Not all feelings are detected by the same nerve endings. In the skin there are 16,000 that detect heat and cold and more than four million that detect pain. Still others cause the sensation of touch. This latter sensation is in some way heightened by the hairs of the body. If a hairy portion of the body is shaved, its sensitivity to touch is temporarily reduced.

Sensations of feeling within the body are difficult to explain. Gas that distends the intestine during an attack of indigestion may cause intense pain. Yet surgeons have found that they can cut, burn, pinch and mash the internal organs of a person without causing the patient any pain.

Are all areas of the skin equally sensitive to the touch? Blindfold yourself. Ask someone to press lightly the blunt point of a pencil on the upturned palm of your hand. Have him repeat this action, using the points of two pencils held about a quarter of an inch apart. Let your helper continue to do this, alternating irregularly between one and two pencil points. As he does this, try to guess how many points are pressing on your hand each time. You will probably make a fairly good score of correct guesses.

But if you repeated this experiment, using the skin of your upper back, close to your spine, you would not be able to tell whether one or two pencil points were being used. This demonstrates that not all areas of the skin are equally sensitive to touch.

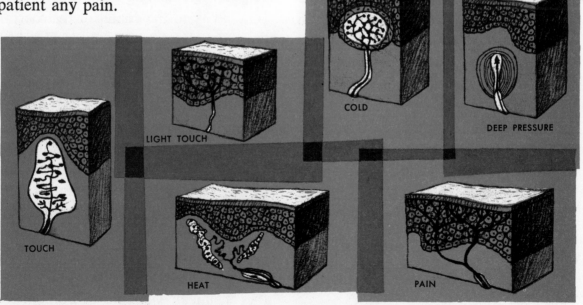

COLD

DEEP PRESSURE

LIGHT TOUCH

TOUCH

HEAT

PAIN

The skin is the organ of feeling. The cross sections show the nerve endings responsible for various sensations.

The Digestive System

We have learned that the blood carries nourishment to the cells of the tissues. This nourishment comes from the food we eat. Certainly, food in the form in which we put it into our mouths could not be carried by the blood. Before food is in a form that enables it to nourish the tissues, it must be greatly changed. This process of change is called *digestion*.

How does the body use food?

The mouth, esophagus (or gullet), stomach, small intestine and large intestine form a continuous tube about thirty feet long called the *alimentary canal*. Food passes through the alimentary canal during the process of digestion. The *liver* and the *pancreas*, two large glands, are also important in the digestion of food. The alimentary canal and these two glands make up the body's *digestive system*.

One of the constituents of food is starch. When food that contains starch is chewed, the saliva in the mouth brings about a chemical change in the starch. As a result of this change, the starch becomes a kind of sugar that is easy for the body to use as nourishment for the cells.

How does digestion begin in the mouth?

A substance, such as saliva, that changes food into a form that can be used by the body is called an *enzyme*. Enzymes are secreted by glands. Saliva is secreted by saliva glands in the roof and floor of the mouth.

Only starch can be digested in the mouth. Fats and proteins, the two other main constituents of food, must be digested farther along in the alimentary canal.

Since food, whether digested in the mouth or other part of the alimentary canal, must be swallowed, the food must first be broken up into small pieces. As we chew, our teeth cut and grind food into small pieces that are wetted by saliva, and finally formed by the tongue into lumps that we can easily swallow.

How do teeth aid digestion?

A tooth is a remarkable structure. The part of the tooth above the gum is the *crown;* below the crown, and covered by the gum, is the *neck;* below the neck is the *root* that lies in the socket of the jaw bone. A tooth has an outside covering of enamel, the hardest material in the body. Inside the enamel, and forming the main part of the tooth, is *dentine*. It looks like bone but is harder. In a cavity in the center of the tooth is the *pulp,* which contains blood vessels and nerves.

When you look on the shelves of a supermarket, you see such a variety of food that it is hard to believe all the different kinds can be divided into a few food elements. But this is true.

What are carbohydrates?

One food element is called *carbohydrate*. Carbohydrates are made up of the chemical elements carbon, hydrogen and oxygen. Starches and sugars, bread and macaroni and rock candy, too, are some carbohydrates. The human body uses carbohydrates as a source of energy. If the body has more carbohydrates than it can use, it may change them into fat, which it stores.

Another food element is *fat,* which is

What is fat?

a better source of energy than carbohydrate. Butter, margarine, lard and olive oil are a few examples of fat as well as the white irregular streaks in a beefsteak and around the edges of the steak.

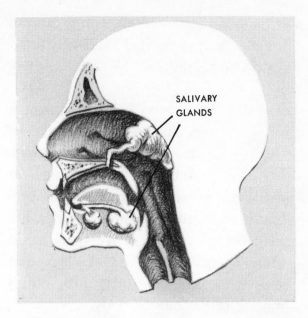

Location of the salivary glands in the human body.

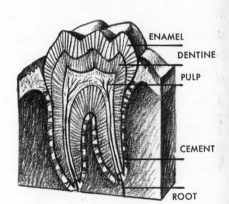

Cross section of a tooth.

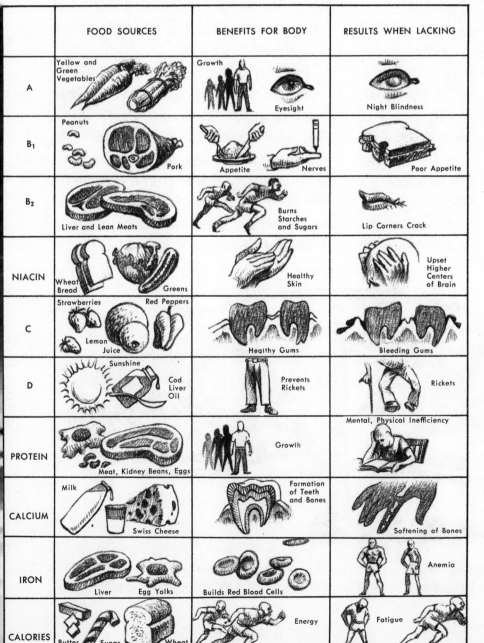

	FOOD SOURCES	BENEFITS FOR BODY	RESULTS WHEN LACKING
A	Yellow and Green Vegetables	Growth / Eyesight	Night Blindness
B₁	Peanuts / Pork	Appetite / Nerves	Poor Appetite
B₂	Liver and Lean Meats	Burns Starches and Sugars	Lip Corners Crack
NIACIN	Wheat Bread / Greens	Healthy Skin	Upset Higher Centers of Brain
C	Strawberries / Red Peppers / Lemon Juice	Healthy Gums	Bleeding Gums
D	Sunshine / Cod Liver Oil	Prevents Rickets	Rickets
PROTEIN	Meat, Kidney Beans, Eggs	Growth	Mental, Physical Inefficiency
CALCIUM	Milk / Swiss Cheese	Formation of Teeth and Bones	Softening of Bones
IRON	Liver / Egg Yolks	Builds Red Blood Cells	Anemia
CALORIES	Butter / Sugar / Wheat Bread	Energy	Fatigue

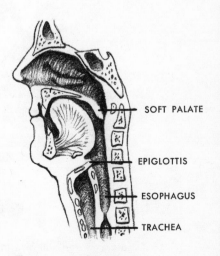

The process of swallowing.

SOFT PALATE

EPIGLOTTIS

ESOPHAGUS

TRACHEA

31

If the body has more fat than it can use for energy, it stores it. That is why some people are stout.

The third main food element is *protein*

What is protein? which is manufactured in the bodies of green plants. When human beings or cattle eat green plants, the plant protein is changed into muscle. When human beings eat meat, which is cattle muscle, they make use of their best source of protein. Meat, also, builds muscle in the human body.

Many foods contain small amounts of

What are vitamins? substances called *vitamins,* which are necessary to the health of the body. Vitamins are named by means of the letters A, B, C, D, and K.

Vitamin A is important for healthy eyes, skin, mucous membranes and for normal growth. Vitamin B is needed for good appetite, good digestion of carbohydrates, normal growth and health of nerves and muscles. Vitamin C is important for growth, the development of teeth, good skin and healing. Vitamin D is needed for strong bones and teeth. Vitamin K is important for the clotting of blood and normal liver function.

Even if we eat enough food, we will not be healthy unless the food contains sufficient vitamins.

Other food elements are called *min-*

What are minerals? *erals.* These are small amounts of certain chemical elements. For example, the elements phosphorus and calcium are needed for healthy teeth and bones.

In order to be healthy, we must give our bodies proper amounts of these food elements. How are we to know just what foods will provide the right amounts? Scientists have worked out the answers, and when our diet includes the proper amounts of each food element, we are then said to be eating a *balanced diet.*

A balanced diet will give the body the nourishment it needs. This is a requirement to maintain good health. A diet that is lacking in certain requirements could lead to a state of unhealth which doctors call *malnutrition.*

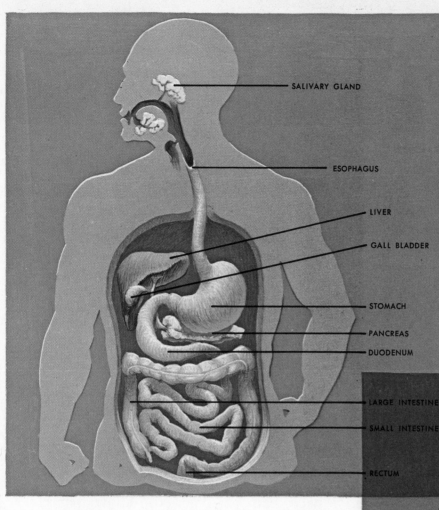

SALIVARY GLAND

ESOPHAGUS

LIVER

GALL BLADDER

STOMACH

PANCREAS

DUODENUM

LARGE INTESTINE

SMALL INTESTINE

RECTUM

The alimentary canal (including the mouth, esophagus, stomach, small and large intestines), the liver and the pancreas make up the body's digestive system.

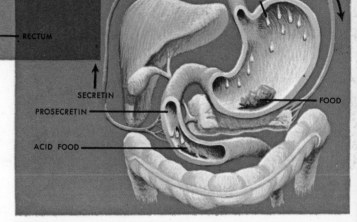

ACID

SECRETIN

SECRETIN

PROSECRETIN

ACID FOOD

FOOD

The stomach and intestine in the digestive process.

Digested food is absorbed through threadlike villi.

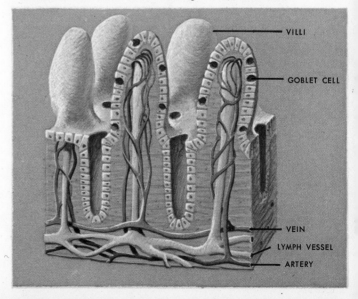

VILLI

GOBLET CELL

VEIN

LYMPH VESSEL

ARTERY

A chicken sandwich, for example, contains starch, fat and protein. The bread is mainly starch, the butter is fat and the chicken is protein.

What is the process of digestion?

When a piece of the sandwich is chewed, the starch is being digested by saliva.

When a mouthful of the sandwich is swallowed, it passes into the *esophagus*. This is the muscular tube that contracts along its length to push the food down into the stomach.

In the stomach, which is a muscle, the food is churned about while digestive juices pour in from glands in the stomach wall. Eventually, the churning action moves food out of the stomach and into the small intestine.

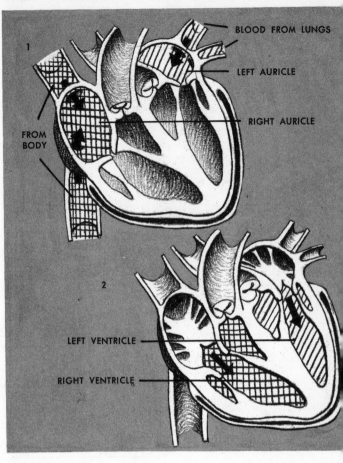

What does the small intestine do? The greater part of the digestive process takes place in the small intestine. Here the protein and the fat are finally changed into forms that can be used by the tissues. The liver contributes to this digestive process by secreting into the small intestine a liquid called *bile*. The pancreas secretes pancreatic juice which further aids in dissolving food.

The small intestine undergoes continual muscular contraction called *peristalsis*. This action pushes the digested food into the large intestine. The surface of the large intestine has a large number of threadlike projections called *villi*. The digested, liquefied food is absorbed through the villi, and passes into capillaries that are inside the villi. Now, the food is in the bloodstream. As we have learned, the blood carries the food to the cells in the tissues, which use the food to provide the body with energy and material for repair.

Not all the parts of the chicken sandwich can be digested. Those parts which are indigestible pass through the large intestine to its lower part, called the *rectum*. Eventually, the indigestible food is eliminated from the rectum through the *anus*.

The Circulatory System

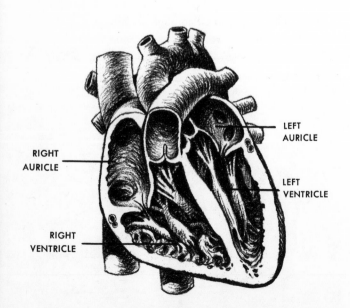

What work does the heart do? Although the study of anatomy is more than 2,000 years old, it was not until the English physician William Harvey described the circulation of the blood, at the beginning of the 17th century, that men knew what work the *heart* did in the body. The heart had been carefully dissected and described, yet no one knew its use.

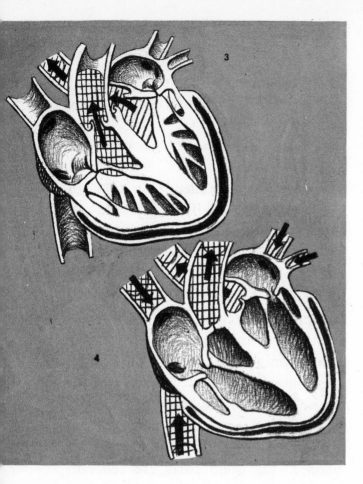

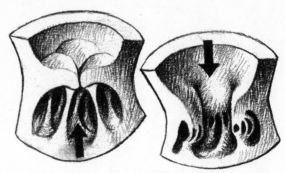

The arrows indicate the direction of blood pressure. Pressure forces closing and opening of the valves.

(1) Auricles contract, squeezing blood into ventricles. (2) Ventricles contract, cuspid valves close, semilunar valves open, blood goes to arteries. (3) Ventricles relax, semilunar valves close, cuspid valves open, blood goes to ventricles. (4) Blood goes to auricles and ventricles, heart relaxes, pauses momentarily.

The heart is a very efficient pump that moves blood through the body. The heart is a muscle that contracts and relaxes about seventy times a minute, for all the minutes of all the years of your life. Each contraction and relaxation of the heart muscle is a *heartbeat*. You have more than 100,000 heartbeats every day. Each heartbeat pumps about two ounces of blood. This results in about 13,000 quarts of blood being pumped each day.

What does the heart look like? The heart is divided into four chambers. The upper two chambers are called *auricles;* the lower two are called *ventricles.* Each auricle is connected with the ventricle below it by a valve that allows blood to flow from the auricle to the ventricle, but not in the opposite direction.

The heart contains a network of nerves that do a remarkable job of regulating its activities. For example, if the heartbeat is weak, the nerves cause the heart muscle to contract more rapidly, thereby pumping an amount of blood equal to that pumped by a strong heartbeat. What is more, not all the areas of the heart take part in every heartbeat. Because of this, parts of the heart are always resting. This is why the heart can continue to beat ceaselessly all during your lifetime.

How can you hear a heartbeat? Obtain two small funnels and a length of rubber tubing about one or two feet long. Into each end of the tube, place the snout of one of the funnels.

Now, place the rim of one funnel on the chest of a friend, and place the other funnel to your ear. The "lub-dupp, lub-dupp, lub-dupp" you hear is the sound of your friend's heart opening and closing. A doctor listens to the heartbeat by using a stethoscope.

Blood has been called "the river of life." This is an appropriate description, because

What work does the blood do?

the blood supplies the cells of the body with the materials they need for nourishment and repair, and it removes wastes from the cells. In addition, the blood contains cells that fight disease and substances that repair cut or bruised parts of the body.

The blood is made up of both liquid and solid parts. The liquid is called *plasma*. The solid parts are *red corpuscles, white corpuscles* and *platelets*.

The heart, blood, veins and arteries make up the circulatory system. The aorta carries the blood from the heart, which branch arteries distribute through body.

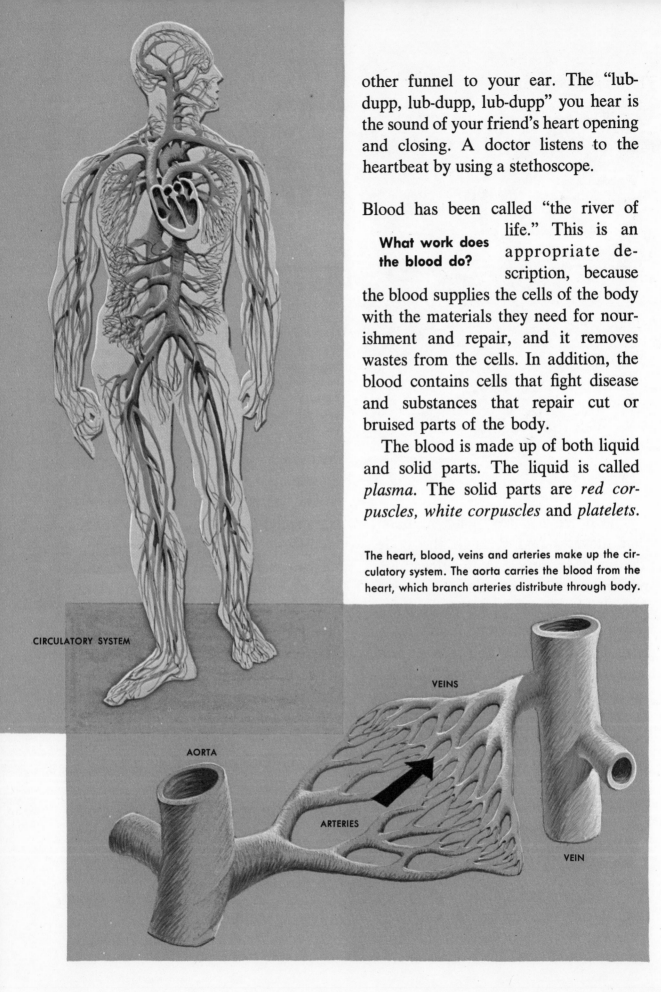

CIRCULATORY SYSTEM

VEINS

AORTA

ARTERIES

VEIN

The word *corpuscle* is the Latin word for "little body."

More than nine-tenths of the blood con-

What are red corpuscles? sists of red corpuscles. They are so small that a large drop of blood contains more than 250 million of them. They are disc-shaped and concave on each side. These corpuscles contain a substance called *hemoglobin,* which is a compound of iron. Hemoglobin can combine very well with oxygen from the air in the lungs. It is the task of the red corpuscles to carry oxygen to cells in all parts of the body, and upon reaching these cells, to give up the oxygen to them.

When hemoglobin combines with oxygen, it turns bright red. That is why blood running out of a cut is always red — the hemoglobin is combining with the oxygen of the air.

Red corpuscles live only about fifty to seventy days, and thus, they must be replaced continuously. We learned that the interior of a bone contains reddish tissue, which is due to the presence of red blood cells. Within the marrow of some bones, red cells are formed.

If a person lacks sufficient red cor-

Red corpuscles, white corpuscles and platelets make up the solid part of the blood, as opposed to plasma.

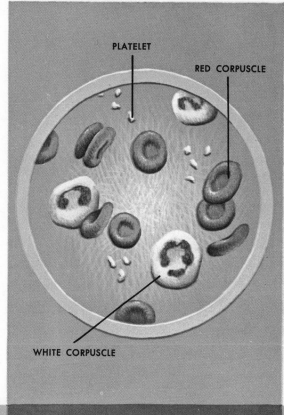

PLATELET

RED CORPUSCLE

WHITE CORPUSCLE

The cross sections, below, demonstrate how the human body uses its own substances to heal surface wounds.

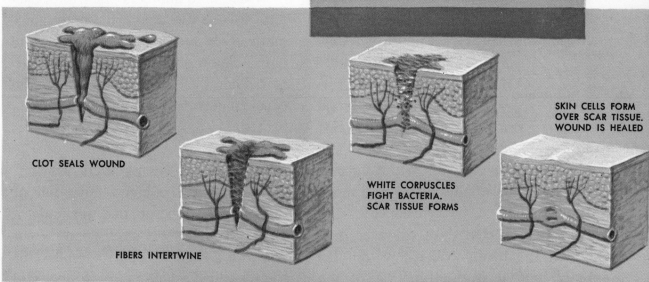

CLOT SEALS WOUND

FIBERS INTERTWINE

WHITE CORPUSCLES FIGHT BACTERIA. SCAR TISSUE FORMS

SKIN CELLS FORM OVER SCAR TISSUE. WOUND IS HEALED

37

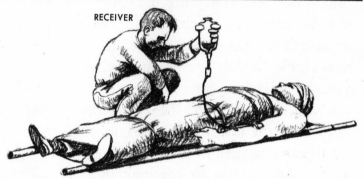

DONOR		RECEIVER		
O	🤝 handshake	🤝 handshake	🤝 handshake	🤝 handshake
AB	⚔ crossed swords	⚔ crossed swords	🤝 handshake	⚔ crossed swords
B	⚔ crossed swords	🤝 handshake	🤝 handshake	⚔ crossed swords
A	🤝 handshake	⚔ crossed swords	🤝 handshake	⚔ crossed swords
	A	B	AB	O

A Nobel prize-winning scientist, Karl Landsteiner, discovered that there were four main groups of blood in humans, which he classified as A, B, AB and O. This is important because in a blood transfusion, a person with one kind of blood would become ill if he received another kind that did not agree with him. The chart shows which blood types can be given in transfusion to persons with any of the four blood groups. It also shows the type of blood that persons with any of the four blood groups can receive. The symbol of the handshake stands for "agree with." The crossed swords signify "opposed to." All the races have the same four blood types.

puscles, he is said to have the disease *anemia*. He is usually listless and thin, because his cells do not receive enough oxygen. Some types of anemia may be cured by adding sufficient iron to an anemic person's diet.

Most white corpuscles are larger than red ones, and there are fewer white corpuscles in the blood than red ones. For approximately every 800 red cells there is only one white cell. White corpuscles have no definite shape, and move about by changing their shape.

How does the blood fight disease?

Disease is caused by an overabundance of harmful bacteria within the body, and it is the function of the white corpuscles to destroy bacteria. To destroy a bacterium, a white cell moves over to the bacterium and then engulfs it. Once the bacterium is inside the white cell, it is digested.

When large numbers of harmful bacteria invade the blood, the body automatically increases the number of white corpuscles produced by the bone marrow. Then the body has sufficient white cells to destroy most of the invading bacteria.

You know that when you cut yourself, the blood flows out of the wound for only a short time. Then the cut fills with a reddish solid material. This solid is called a *blood clot*. If blood did

How does blood clot?

not clot, anyone with even a slight wound would bleed profusely. Indeed, the blood of certain persons does not clot, a condition known as *hemophilia*.

The platelets are the particles in the blood responsible for causing it to clot. When blood flows from a cut, it carries platelets. When air comes into contact with the platelets, the oxygen in the air causes the platelets to disintegrate and release a substance that combines with certain substances in the plasma. This combination forms a substance called *fibrin*. Fibrin is in the form of a network of tiny threadlike fibers that trap the cells of the blood to form a dam which holds back the further flow of blood.

Since the heart pumps so much blood, it must be clear that the same blood must pass through the heart many times in the course of a day. This is true, for the round trip of blood from the heart to distant parts of the body and back takes less than a minute. The round trip to nearer parts of the body takes an even shorter time.

How does blood move through the body?

The blood takes two main paths in its trip through the body. When the right ventricle of the heart contracts, blood is forced into a large artery that leads to the lungs. (An *artery* is an elastic tube that carries blood away from the heart.) Here the red cells of the blood take up oxygen from the air in the lungs. They also give up carbon dioxide.

From the lungs, the blood flows through two veins that lead back to the heart. (A *vein* is an elastic tube that carries blood toward the heart.) The blood enters the left auricle and passes through the valve leading to the left ventricle. When the left ventricle contracts, the blood flows into another large artery. This artery branches into smaller arteries that branch several times more into smaller and smaller arteries. The smallest arteries are in the tissues, and are called *capillary* arteries. From the capillaries, the blood transfers nourishment and oxygen to the cells and removes carbon dioxide and other wastes.

Capillary arteries connect with capillary veins. These tiny veins connect with larger and larger veins as they approach nearer to the heart. Blood flowing through the veins eventually reaches a large vein that enters the right auricle of the heart. From the right auricle, the blood flows through the valve leading to the right ventricle, and thus it ends a complete round trip through the body.

The heart, the blood and the veins and arteries make up the body's *circulatory system*.

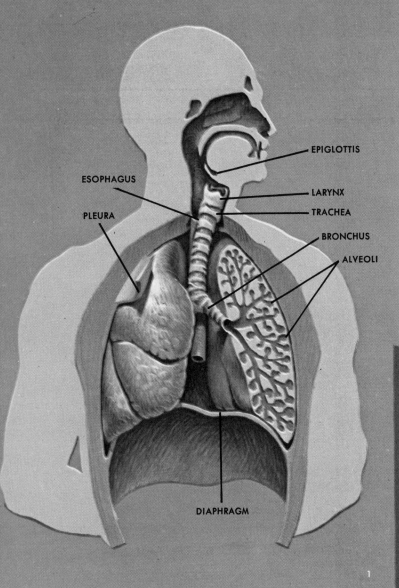

ESOPHAGUS

PLEURA

EPIGLOTTIS

LARYNX

TRACHEA

BRONCHUS

ALVEOLI

DIAPHRAGM

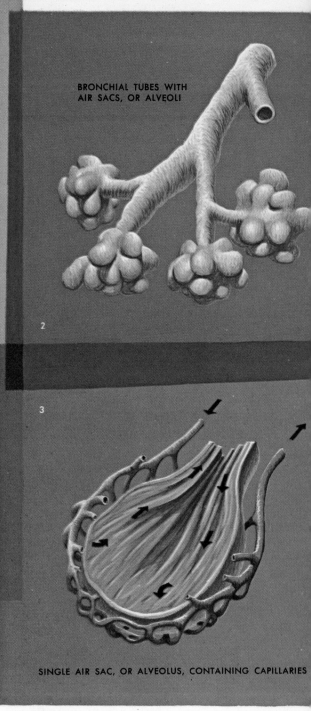

BRONCHIAL TUBES WITH AIR SACS, OR ALVEOLI

2

3

SINGLE AIR SAC, OR ALVEOLUS, CONTAINING CAPILLARIES

1. Respiratory system. 2. Bronchial tubes with alveoli. 3. Alveolus; as per arrows, oxygen enters blood, carbon dioxide passes out. 4. Passage of oxygen and carbon dioxide through body. 5. Expiration (breathing out); lungs contract, ribs move down. 6. Inspiration (breathing in); lungs expand, ribs move up.

The Respiratory System

Why do we breathe? We have learned that the cells of the body need oxygen, and that the oxygen is obtained from the air. In order to obtain oxygen, we must first get air into our bodies, which we do by inhaling, or breathing in.

Across the body cavity, and below the lungs, is a flat, powerful muscle called the *diaphragm*. When this muscle is moved downward, it causes the ribs to move upward and outward. The result is a partial vacuum that is produced in the lungs. The pressure of the

40

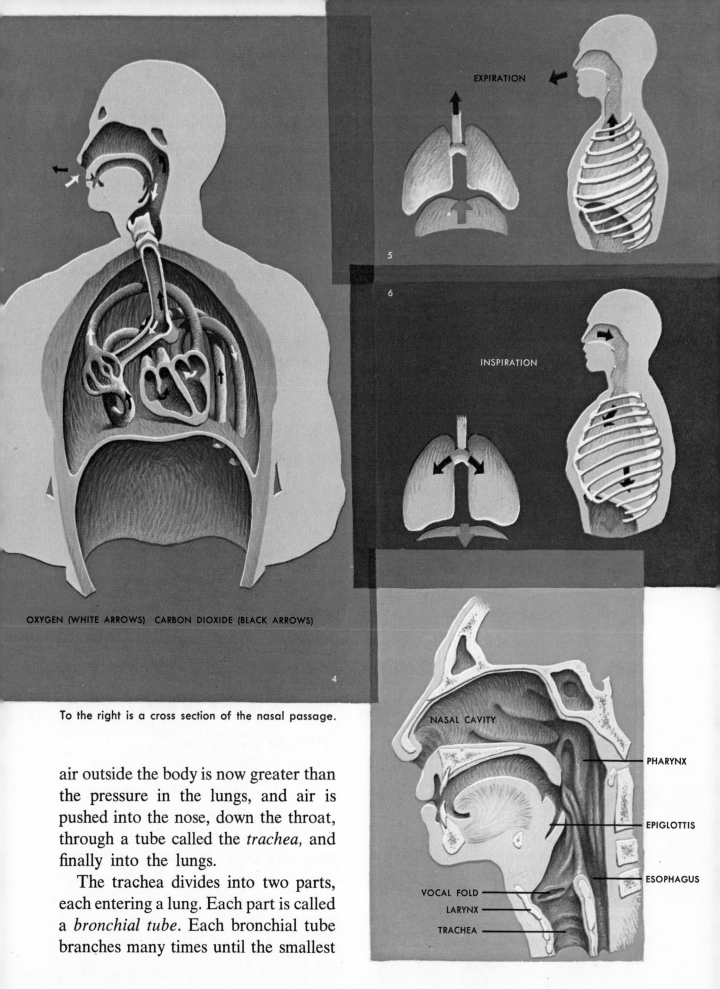

OXYGEN (WHITE ARROWS) CARBON DIOXIDE (BLACK ARROWS)

EXPIRATION

INSPIRATION

NASAL CAVITY

PHARYNX

EPIGLOTTIS

ESOPHAGUS

VOCAL FOLD

LARYNX

TRACHEA

To the right is a cross section of the nasal passage.

air outside the body is now greater than the pressure in the lungs, and air is pushed into the nose, down the throat, through a tube called the *trachea*, and finally into the lungs.

The trachea divides into two parts, each entering a lung. Each part is called a *bronchial tube*. Each bronchial tube branches many times until the smallest

41

branches are almost as small as capillaries. These smallest branches are called *alveoli*. The tissues that make up the alveoli contain capillary arteries and veins.

Oxygen passes from the air through the walls of the arteries, and combines with the red blood cells. Carbon dioxide passes through the walls of the veins, and into the air in the lungs.

When the diaphragm relaxes, the ribs move downward, compress the lungs, and force the carbon-dioxide-rich air out of the lungs by the same path through which it entered.

To do this, you must obtain a bell jar,

How can you make a model breathing apparatus?

a one-hole rubber stopper that will fit the jar, a glass tube in the shape of a Y, two small balloons and a large thin piece of rubber.

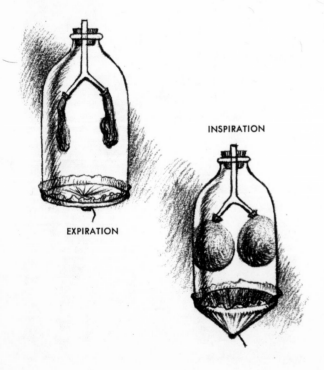

INSPIRATION

EXPIRATION

Place the stopper in the mouth of the jar. Tie the two balloons to the ends of the arms of the Y-tube. Put the other end of the glass tube into the hole in the stopper, doing so by way of the bottom of the bell jar. Tie the large piece of rubber around the bottom of the bell jar.

By pulling downward on the bottom of the large piece of rubber, which represents the diaphragm, you will simulate the breathing process. The upper part of the tube represents the trachea, the arms represent the bronchial tubes, and the balloons represent the lungs.

One way that the cells of the body use

How is air important to the body cells?

the nourishment brought to them by the blood is in providing energy for the body's movements. To provide this energy, certain parts of the nourishment stored in the cells must be combined with oxygen. The oxygen is obtained from the air through the breathing process, and is taken to the cells by the red corpuscles.

When you run you use up more energy.

Why do you breathe more deeply when you run?

This energy must come from the combination of oxygen with the stored nourishment in the cells. The process of combination must take place on a larger scale than usual. To bring this about you need more oxygen in your blood. By breathing more deeply you get more oxygen in your lungs and, thereby, more oxygen in your blood.

The Excretory System

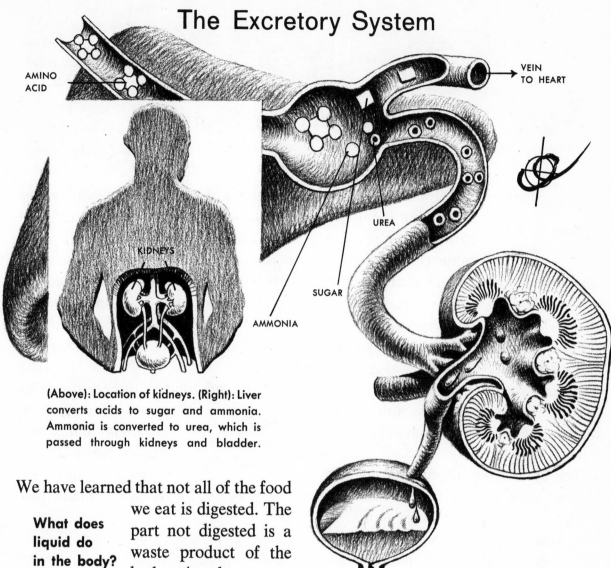

AMINO ACID

VEIN TO HEART

KIDNEYS

UREA

SUGAR

AMMONIA

(Above): Location of kidneys. (Right): Liver converts acids to sugar and ammonia. Ammonia is converted to urea, which is passed through kidneys and bladder.

We have learned that not all of the food we eat is digested. The part not digested is a waste product of the body. Another waste product about which we have learned is the air which contains carbon dioxide.

What does liquid do in the body?

We drink many liquids, some of which provide us with nourishment. Milk is such a liquid. The foods we eat are largely water. The water is quite useful, because, upon entering the bloodstream, it keeps the nourishing food materials dissolved so that they can pass through the membranes of the cells of tissues. It also dissolves waste products within the cells. Somehow, the plasma of the blood, which is partly water, must get rid of the dissolved waste products.

This task is performed by the *kidneys* which are at the lower part of the back, above the hips. Each kidney contains millions of tiny coiled tubes. Blood flows through these tubes and the liquid waste products in the blood are filtered out. These liquid wastes pass from the kidney into a sac where they are temporarily stored. This storage sac is the *bladder*. Every so often, your bladder becomes sufficiently full so as to cause you to want to empty it, a process called *urination*.

How do the kidneys help us?

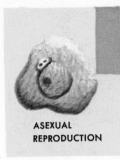

ASEXUAL
REPRODUCTION

The Reproductive System

How do cells reproduce?

Living things can reproduce themselves, but nonliving things cannot. A stone can be broken into several pieces; and each piece is permanently smaller than the original stone. Living things reproduce other things that closely resemble the parent. Dogs reproduce themselves as puppies that grow into dogs. Human beings reproduce themseves as babies that grow into adult humans much like their parents.

The unit of reproduction is the unit of the body — the cell. Within the body, cells are continuously reproducing themselves. After a cell has lived for a certain length of time, changes take place within its cytoplasm. These changes soon cause the cell to begin to narrow at the middle. Eventually, the narrowing process pinches the cell into two cells. But the changes in the cytoplasm have made certain that each new cell has all the parts a cell needs in order to live and function. The new cells soon grow to the size of their parent cell. Then the new cells split in two.

What is the process of reproduction?

Human and animal reproduction begins with single cells. A female animal has within her body, in a special sac, cells called *egg cells*. A male animal pro-

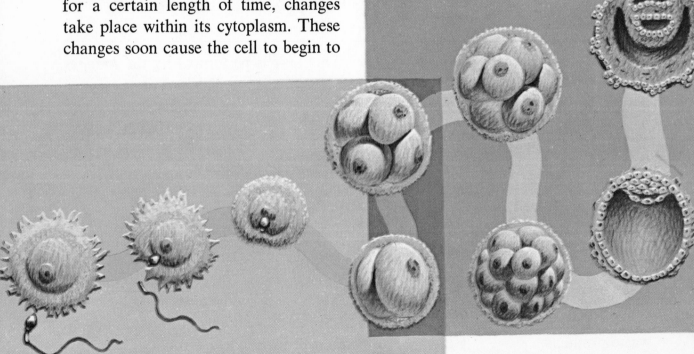

duces in his body certain cells called *sperm cells.*

If a sperm cell comes in contact with an egg cell, the sperm cell is absorbed by the egg cell. This absorption causes the egg cell to begin to reproduce itself by splitting in two. This splitting process goes on until the original egg cell has become thousands of cells.

These thousands of cells form a hollow ball. As reproduction of the cells in the ball continues, one side of the ball caves inward, creating a double-walled hemisphere.

Up until now, the cells in the hemisphere have all seemed to be of the same kind. Now, as the reproduction of cells continues, different types of

Human beings produce children by the process of reproduction. When a sperm cell, the male sex cell, joins with an egg, the female sex cell, the egg becomes fertilized. The fertilized egg develops into billions of cells that form an embryo, which is the name given to a baby during its first few months of development in the mother's body. Later, the developing infant is called a fetus. It takes about nine months for a child to be born. This nine-month period is known as pregnancy or the gestation period.

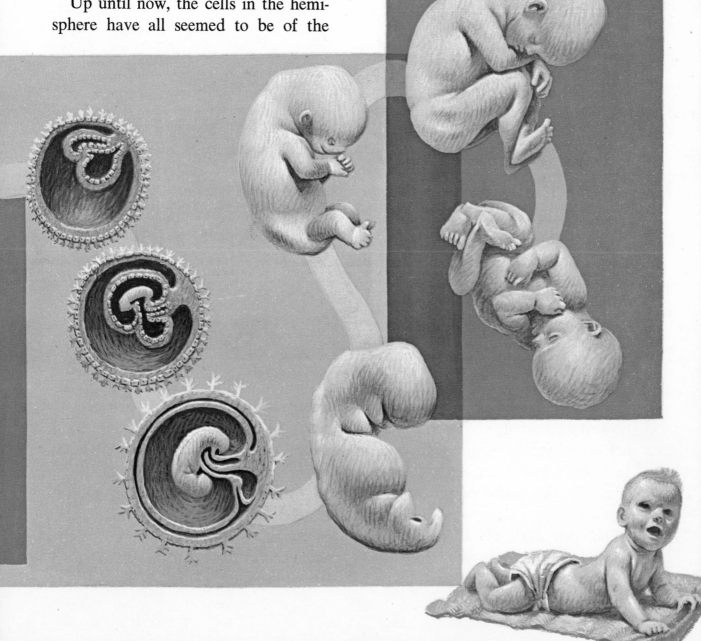

cells form in different parts of the new living thing. In other words, tissues begin to form.

The process of the reproduction of cells in mammals may go on for many months. During this time, what was once a ball of cells begins to form all the parts of the animal's body.

This whole process takes place in the body of the mother animal. The part of her body that holds the newly-forming animal is called the *uterus*. At last, a whole small animal has been formed as the result of continuous cell reproduction. When this time arrives, the muscles of the uterus contract, and the fully-formed little animal is pushed out of the uterus — that is, it is born.

In human beings, the complete process of reproducing a new human being — a baby — takes just a little over nine months.

Your Body and Your Person

We have learned about the parts of the body-machine. When all these parts are put together, we not only have a human body, but also a person.

Why is the human body more than a machine?

What makes us a person is nothing that we can see or touch. It is the fact that we love and want to be loved, have ideas, plan things, daydream, feel sorrow and pity — in short, to do the things that make you human.

Suppose that you and a friend were both hungry, and then you came upon a small amount of food. If you were to act only like a machine satisfying its fuel needs, you would eat all the food yourself. However, since you are a human being, as well as a human machine, you share the food with your friend, even though your fuel needs may not be completely met.

When a machine is fueled, it works until it needs more fuel. The human machine not only does this, but it plans ahead for the time when there will be no more fuel. In other words, human beings know their food will run out, so they plant crops, hunt and fish.

Human beings have *emotions*. It is not easy to say just what an emotion is, but love, hate, sadness, happiness, anger and tenderness are some emotions. All human beings have emotional needs — the need to experience certain emotions. All persons need to be loved, to feel a little bit important, to feel needed and to have new experiences. Attempts to satisfy these needs are the main things that spur human beings to act as they do.

What are emotions?

Care of the Body

Need for exercise: Everyone needs some exercise in order to keep the muscles in good condition. When we remember how much of the body is made up of muscles, we realize the importance of this conditioning. The object of exercise is to cause the heart to pump a little faster. This forces a little more blood into capillaries in the tissues, and makes certain that every part of the body is being nourished and having its waste products removed. It also causes deeper breathing, thereby emptying out carbon dioxide from sacs in the lungs that are ordinarily not used.

The right amount of exercise gives a feeling of well-being, not fatigue.

". . . All work and no play makes Jack a dull boy . . ."

Need for rest: Very strenuous exercise or exercising for too long may produce fatigue. Fatigue is caused by wastes accumulating in the body. When muscles are moving continuously or are under strain, they produce more waste products than the body can immediately rid itself of. When this happens, the body needs rest, in order to catch up on waste removal. Sleep is the best kind of rest and one should get enough sleep every day.

Care of the skin: There are many skin diseases, some of which are caused by germs. Others are due to substances to which the skin is very sensitive. For example, boils are caused by an infection of certain bacteria commonly found on the skin. Fungus growths can also cause skin diseases. Dirty, neglected skin can result in infestation by insects, such as lice.

A clean skin will either completely eliminate the possibility of these skin ailments, or will lessen the presence of the things that cause them, to the point where the natural protective functions of the body can handle such threats.

The skin should be thoroughly washed with mild soap at least once a day. If an infection or a fungus growth does take place, a physician should be consulted.

Care of the eyes: The eyes are probably the most valuable sense organs. They should not be exposed to very bright sunlight. In the presence of bright sunlight, sunglasses give adequate protection.

One should always have sufficient

light when reading or writing. Rest the eyes occasionally by looking into the distance or by closing them once in a while.

Never rub the eyes with dirty towels or hands. An infection may result.

The eyes should be tested regularly — at least once a year, or more frequently as the case may be — by an eye doctor.

Above all, never try to treat any eye trouble yourself. Always obtain the help of a physician.

Care of the hair and nails: Those who have healthy skin will probably also have healthy hair and nails. Hair can be kept clean only by washing, and a thorough shampoo once a week is usually sufficient. But if the hair is particularly oily, it may have to be washed more often. Brushing the hair frequently stimulates the circulation in the scalp, and also helps to remove dirt, loose hairs and dandruff.

Most dandruff is not a disease. The outer layer of the skin naturally flakes off, and these flakes may cause mild dandruff. However, if the scalp is also very oily and reddened, it may indicate the kind of dandruff that requires the help of a physician.

If the nails dry and split easily, proper food elements in the diet may be lacking. A balanced diet frequently clears up this condition.

Care of the ears: Never poke any hard object into the ear — it may break the eardrum. Glands in the ear secrete a substance called ear wax. The purpose of this secretion is to keep the eardrum pliable. Sometimes these glands secrete too much wax, which blocks up the ear canal and impairs the hearing. If this happens, do not try to remove the wax yourself. Get the help of a doctor.

Keep the ears clean by washing them with soap and water, and use nothing sharper than a finger to wash in the opening of the ear canal.

Care of the teeth: Particles of food left in the mouth after a meal provide nourishment for bacteria. Bacteria secrete a substance which can dissolve the enamel of the teeth, and thereby cause cavities. For this reason, the teeth should be brushed after each meal whenever possible. This will remove the food particles, and prevent the action of the bacteria.

Since it is not always possible to prevent all decay, even by regular brushing of the teeth, a dentist should be consulted two or three times a year.

The hygienic care of the body becomes especially meaningful when we remember that good health is largely dependent on a body which functions properly. Good health to you all!

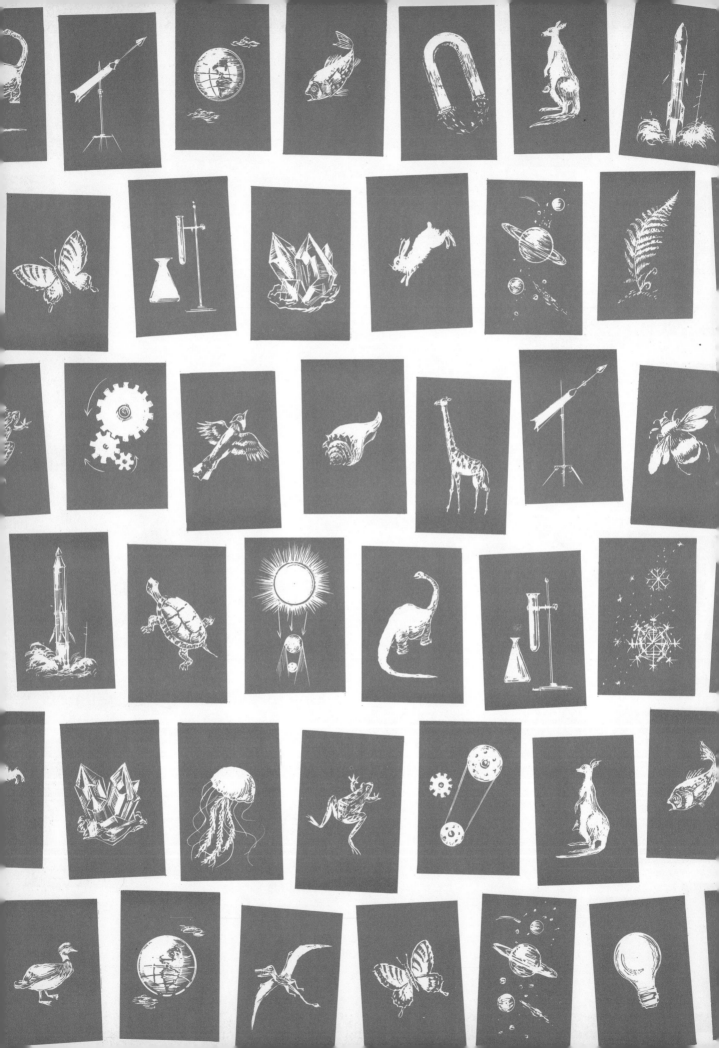